Counselling and Spiritual Direction

Counselling and
Spiritual Direction

David Bick

The Pentland Press Limited
Edinburgh • Cambridge • Durham • USA

© David Bick 1997

First published in 1997 by
The Pentland Press Ltd.
1 Hutton Close
South Church
Bishop Auckland
Durham

British Library Cataloguing in Publication Data.
A catalogue record for this book is available
from the British Library.

ISBN 1 85821 495 5

Typeset by CBS, Felixstowe, Suffolk
Printed and bound by Antony Rowe Ltd., Chippenham

DEDICATION

In our present culture those who offer help to others are seen as experts, or 'superior' people offering something to those who are 'inferior', without any expertise or ability.

My experience has taught me that this is a false and dangerous concept. I have come to see myself as one who has been enriched and taught by those to whom I have made myself available in a helping role, as either pastor, counsellor, or spiritual director. I do indeed have some expertise and my training has given me something as well. I do not despise or deny this, but it is also true that many of those to whom I have offered help, have exposed my weaknesses, pointed me to my continual need of God's grace, and as a result kept me humble enough to avoid many pitfalls, and especially that of professional paranoia.

I would like therefore to acknowledge the contribution of these many people from whom, in the process of seeking to help them, I have gained much myself. Of these I think especially of Yasmin with whom I have shared much pain, prayed much, and from whom I have gained much understanding.

THANK YOU

I would like to thank my wife for her patient support in checking the text for those many silly mistakes I am prone to make, making helpful suggestions, and generally keeping me 'on track'. As well as this I am also grateful to my friends and colleagues for their encouragements, gentle cajoling and support, without which I feel I would have begun little and achieved less.

Contents

Part One

The Counsellor's Relationship with God

Chapter I

The Christian Counsellor

What is a Christian counsellor? Simply a Christian person who counsels. All the insights and techniques of the secular counselling world are valid for the Christian counsellor if they are based on accurate observation. This is so because of the incarnation. In St John's Gospel Chapter 1, we are told that the 'Word', namely Jesus, became flesh and lived amongst us. As the whole world is God's creation, the very act of Jesus Christ entering into it as an ordinary human gave God's seal of approval to human life for our benefit. If therefore, observation of human life provides insights and techniques that are useful for the counsellor as he or she tries to help others to a fuller life, they must be seen to be of God, even if the person who observes them claims to be an atheist. God is not so small that he who created it all in the first place can be limited by the attitudes of one of his own creation. The danger of the secular approach lies in inaccurate observation and making the observation the basis of a whole philosophy of life. St Paul says this clearly in Romans Chapter 1 verse 25 'They exchanged the truth of God for a lie and worshipped and served the creature rather than the creator'. The key then to being a Christian counsellor lies in the counsellor's relationship with God the creator. If this is right then grace will be given through the Holy Spirit to enable any insight from secular counselling to be used in an appropriate way.

In a counselling dialogue in which the counsellor is operating from a Christian standpoint, it is the Holy Spirit who does the work. The counsellor's function is to enable the Spirit to work throughout and not get in the way. Therefore the counsellor's relationship with God at the time, in the here and now of the situation, is paramount. The counsellor must be listening in four areas . . . What is God saying? . . . What is the

3

client saying? . . . What is going on inside the client, behind what is being said? . . . and What is going on emotionally inside the counsellor? The counsellor should only make tentative suggestions to guide and stimulate. Beware of the temptation to give ready made answers, sound doctrine at a shallow intellectual level, or to manipulate emotionally. Quick and easy answers block the work of the Spirit, and the desire to give them is a sign of anxiety and faithlessness in the counsellor.

Most people today are so full of hang-ups and spiritually empty that it will take years to sort them out. Because we live in a collapsing society that is based on materialism, many people become Christians because they are looking for something more real and durable than they have yet experienced. The Devil will hook them on the modern vice of everything being instant. When the Spirit brings out the inner diseases of the soul, life becomes so painful that many give up. The Christian counsellor must be committed to clients long enough to work through these things. Counselling is not about smoothing over or taking away emotional pain, it is about exposing it so that the Holy Spirit can give grace to work through it; in this the Gospel is opposed to the spirit of the age.

It must be said that counselling is more complicated than people think, and its pitfalls are many. It cannot be taught out of books or by quick and easy methods. If you think that God may be calling you to this ministry, don't dabble, do three things. Firstly strengthen your spiritual life with a real commitment to prayer. Secondly, get a good training course in counselling, this will take several years. Thirdly, get someone mature and able to give you guidance, supervision and spiritual direction, thus enabling you to check out where you are spiritually and to keep you moving in the right direction. This also must be a long-term commitment.

Why Christian Counselling?
'Why is it necessary to pay attention to this? Why can't we just get on with giving people practical down to earth help as and when they ask for it?' are questions often asked. Theologians, ie people who talk about God, are often seen as people who are not very practical in an age when 'Getting on with the job', achieving things in a material concrete form, and being active are in fashion. Yet, when one pauses to take a deeper

look at the times in which we live, an aware person soon senses that it is a superficial, neurotic and frightened age.

This is indicative of an age that has lost contact with God in a meaningful way. He has been distanced from personal experience so that to most people he has become just another theory about the nature of things. A counsellor who wishes to offer any real and lasting help must come to know and experience God as a living reality, who is personal, and able to act in love in every possible human situation. It is only extending the falseness of our age and playing along with its deceit if counsellors who claim to be Christian merely offer those in trouble just another fashionable straw. Neither must they offer themselves as being a sufficient source of strength for coping with life in this troubled world. The Christian counsellor must be set upon something sound, tested and reliable, and also be able to point clients to it at an appropriate time for them. Psalm 61 verse 2 says, 'Set me upon the rock that is higher than I'. This rock is God as revealed to us through Christ. It is to the issues involved in sustaining a relationship with the living God through the revelation of Christ that we now turn.

The first thing we need to remember is that the initiative in our relationship with God lies with God. Our side of the relationship is to recognise God's action towards us and to respond to it. In the first stages we are largely passive and God active. This is difficult to understand, because there is a degree of activity even in response, but our nature is such that we think too easily in terms of 'finding God' rather than allowing him to 'find us'. By doing this we block the work of the Spirit and isolate ourselves within our own futile activity. The harder we try, the worse things seem to become.

The second thing to remember is that God is both the means and the end of our endeavour. The story of the wise men in St Matthew Chapter 2 illustrates this point. God, who revealed himself through Jesus was the end of their journey. The star was given by God as a means by which he led them to a relationship with himself through Jesus. The symbolism of the gifts they brought showed how the Holy Spirit had revealed to them what the babe in the manger was really about. The fact that they were able to be warned in a dream of the dangers in going back to Herod

5

shows how open they were in being guided by God. It was the committed, trusting, persevering openness shown by these people to God that led them on towards the truth. They are, I believe, a practical example of the maxim of St Augustine, 'I believe, in order that I might understand'.

The third important point is the 'Lordship of Christ'. The Gospel states that God has put Jesus in command of all things and that he will always have the victory in the end. Once we have therefore committed ourselves to 'being Christian' nothing that happens can separate us from the love of God no matter how horrific it may seem to us. This is not only important to us in time of trial, but to those whom we may counsel. A most important factor in helping others is making them feel safe with us. The counsellor must be able to do this and stay with all the pain of the person being counselled. If the counsellor has a wellbeing that comes from actively trusting God and really believing in the Lordship of Christ, then this gives a stability that the troubled person senses, thereby enabling them more easily to open up the painful areas that had previously been repressed. In cases where the counsellor is lacking this trust in God, mainly due to their own deficiency of experience in the reality of God and his ways, it is inevitable that the growth potential for the counsellee becomes greatly restricted. It is reduced to that which the counsellor can cope with in purely human terms, because in such a situation the abundant flow of God's grace becomes blocked. Thus, having seen the basic need for the Christian counsellor's real and developing relationship with God, let now us examine that relationship in more detail.

Knowing God

God must be known and experienced personally if the counsellor is to have any real stability or to be able to love and stay with the pain of others. The love that heals is the one that is given without any strings attached. It is unconditional. This is the love God shows us in Christ. When we receive Christ and allow him to rule in our hearts we become a new creation, a new person. We then know God through Christ living in us. As we shall see later, this touches our whole life; our intellect, our emotions, our imagination, our will, our conscience. Our response to the Gospel means that we are no longer conditioned by fashion and the world, but by Christ with us and the word of God. This does not happen quickly. It is a slowly growing process which needs tending and directing. The world still pressurises us and the old Adam within still tries to assert itself. Knowing God through personal experience brings with it a deep peace and inner stability as well as tensions. It is in learning how to come to terms with our whole selves, as we become aware of the good and bad parts of us, and the inner fears this raises, without rejecting any of it, that we put ourselves in a position to receive the grace of God and grow strong in spiritual terms.

Assuming the reader's personal commitment to a relationship with God and their desire to maintain and develop it, we will now look at the rules or guidelines, the problems in applying them and the practical issues arising from that relationship.

The Basic Rules or Guidelines
These are laid down by God and form the basic working framework of our relationship with Him. There are just three of them: one, love God; two, love your neighbour; three, love yourself. These are the basis of the Jewish 'Shema' (see Deuteronomy Chapters 5 and 6, and St Mark Chapter 12, verses 28-34), which is the summary of the law. Jesus himself ratified the importance of these three basic rules in St Luke Chapter 20 verses 25-28 when, in conversation with a lawyer, he told him quite simply that if he obeyed these three rules by living them out he would 'Live'. To be in the right relationship with God is to live fully. When we do this we have a freedom to love and be loved without any strings attached. The theory as stated in these three rules is very simple to grasp with the mind, but very hard to carry out because it involves our whole selves and we are much more than a mind. We all have hidden depths and irrational, unruly parts of our personality that drive us where we do not want to go. These then are the guidelines; what problems arise when we try to apply them?

The Problems Related to the Development of Our Relationship with God
The Biblical view of a human being is that to be human is to be a 'living

soul' (Hebrew Nephesh). This living soul is a unity of many parts all of which must be involved in a relationship. Human beings are made in the image of God. That is, we are made like him and designed so that our truest fulfilment can only come when we are in relationship with him. We are therefore in some ways like God, but in other ways he is different from us. It is these two things together that make it possible for us to have a relationship with him, because we need to have something in common to be able to meet, but also need to be able to be separate from him in order to make the relationship a reality. If we are just an extension of God, or God just an extension of us then no relationship would be possible. If on the other hand God was totally different from us, then there would be no meeting point between God and us, his creatures and, again, no relationship would be possible. This is why Christian Theology always sees God as being both immanent and transcendent. He is at the same time both inside and outside his creation. As we will see in the practical exercises, this doctrine of immanence and transcendence needs to be fully grasped, since it has important implications when it comes to God's guidance.

A healthy relationship between a human being and God has another problematical area. It is that of relating to other people. In no way can anyone be well related to God, but at the same time unrelated to others, because other people are like little mirrors reflecting back to us something of ourselves and also at times something of God. In this aspect, relationships with others are an extension of the transcendent and immanent nature of God as he relates to his creation. This is why our relationship with God can only be developed fully within the fellowship of believers, the local Church.

In any relationship that is healthy, including our relationship with God, there are two basic requirements. The first is commitment, which we need to see as a long term thing, which involves our whole self. The second is a willingness to have our darker side exposed, things in us which when we began we did not recognise as belonging to us. We must accept them as they are and come to terms with whatever way God may choose to deal with them. It is essential that we stay with the pain of this and also keep faithful to our commitment in hard times. It is always good to remember that God is both the objective of our relationship and the one who is with us as we work towards developing it.

Because we as human beings are 'Fearfully and wonderfully made', the giving of ourselves is not easy. We all tend to withhold some parts and by so doing become lop-sided Christians. The lop-sidedness is something which unbalances and causes tensions because as a basic unity all aspects of our personality fuse into each other. It is indeed a mystery, but for convenience we can divide that unity into the five related parts previously mentioned, each one of which is vital to our relationship with God. As we do so, it is necessary to be aware of the limitations of so doing, since the aim is to be practical and avoid the confusion of highly speculative areas.

Intellect

It is by use of our intellect that we are able to understand. The mistake we are tempted to make is that of thinking that we can know by the use of the intellect alone. This is one of the errors of the present time which can trap people into atheism. In our relationship with God the danger is always of misuse of the intellect. At the one extreme, if we overuse it and ignore other aspects of our personality, we become trapped in our own little world of theories. This makes us deny things we do not understand and limits our awareness. It can make us hard, insensitive and very defensive, with an urge to argue about everything and always come to no definite conclusions. In this extreme the intellect cuts us off from God and most of reality. If by overuse of intellect a person does not end up an atheist, he or she will become a narrow religious and 'Pharisaical' person who does not know the living God but who worships his or her own narrow concept of him.

It is possible to become aware of our over reliance on intellect by taking note of the occasions when neat theologically based answers are given, either to explain our own problems or those of a counsellee, which contradict the reality of the situation at the time. These are not always immediately evident, but as time passes an unease wells up within us. It is at the point where we become aware of an unease welling up within us that action needs to be taken by getting in touch with it, praying that the Holy Spirit should give us enlightenment, and then taking whatever action is required. If nothing is done in a non-intellectual way with the unease, the usual response is to work harder to reinforce our 'theology'.

At the other extreme are those who so totally abandon the use of their intellect in their relationship with God that they are driven by every emotion and impulse that they experience, blow hot and cold and are most unstable, attributing to God many things that are not of him. When this mistake is made, those who make it become depressed and resentful, feeling that they are continually being overwhelmed by forces outside themselves, usually demons. There is a tendency for counsellors in such positions to cast out demons where they do not exist. When nothing improves, the depression increases and God becomes remote. Any suggestion that such people might be theologically wrong, or misunderstanding God is resented. Theology itself as a discipline is rejected. Dealing with these two extremes of misuse of the intellect is largely a matter of humility and self awareness. The practical exercises in Chapter II are a means of helping with this, especially exercises (i), (ii) and (iv).

It is clear that by use of intellect alone we cannot know God and without using our intellect we will not be able to develop our relationship with him. It is part of our nature as human beings that we experience things first and think about them afterwards. When we experience God through his love revealed in Christ, then the intellect comes into its own so that we can have an understanding of that experience. Intellect is always secondary to experience, but at the same time essential for us to be able to use and understand our experience.

The importance of our intellect in our relationship with God is that it gives us a yardstick by which we can test the validity of our experience of him. Without this yardstick we are lost. We develop it by knowing the scriptures, knowing the basic doctrines set out in the creeds which sum up the corporate experience of the Christian Church, and learning about the lives of the saints, both past and contemporary. This kind of knowing is intellectual and a valid part of knowing God, but only a part.

Emotions

These are many and powerful. They are the part of us which feels, whereas our intellect thinks. Because the emotions are powerful, hard to understand and at times apparently conflicting, we have a strong desire to avoid owning them as part of us. We either repress them, pretending they do not exist, or project them onto other people or objects, or even make demons of them. This bad handling, or non-recognition of our emotions is very common and is the source of illnesses of all kinds both physical and mental. The root of these illnesses is in fact spiritual because it comes from being out of relationship with God so that we cannot put our trust in him. When we are in a right relationship with God our emotions can be brought into the open with him because we feel safe to be ourselves. It is only possible to look honestly at our emotions and recognise them when we are in a position of safety. It always makes people feel safe when they have a loving accepting relationship with another person who is absolutely trustworthy, be it God or a human being. Psalm 91 states this in a wider sense than just an emotional one.

The positive side of our emotions is that through them we can be made aware of danger or sense other things that our intellect cannot detect. Emotions that are unhealthy see fear where no fear is, or force us to rationalize away emotional danger signals by overuse of the intellect. When this happens in a person they become remote, unaware and easily threatened. In a counsellor, badly handled emotions make the counsellee feel unsafe and also limit the counsellor's ability to pick up and understand what is going on in the counselling dialogue. It is therefore very important that our emotions are treasured and cared for. We do this in the context of developing our relationship with God. Exercise (iv) is especially relevant for this purpose.

Imagination

This is that part of our personality which is able to perceive and understand truths by the means of pictures. These pictures are also deep truths which can be communicated. This is the basis of art which has always had an important part to play in human culture. Dreams are a part of our imaginative processes and it is interesting to note how much they feature in scripture, especially as a means by which God communicates with his servants. For this last reason alone, it is important for us not to neglect the use and development of imagination in our relationship with God. It will be discussed further in a number of the practical exercises.

Will

This is that part of our personality which enables us to make decisions, and assert ourselves so that we can carry them out. It could be said to be an aspect of personality which does not stand on its own, but is the product of a relationship between intellect and emotions. People who have a good intellect but weak, sick or repressed emotions will lack the ability to make decisions or the drive to carry them out, even though they are able to see the issues involved and understand the desirability to take a certain course of action. People with a weak intellect and strong, unbalanced emotions will find themselves driven where they do not want to go and be easily roused, tempted or led astray. In both cases the will is weak because it can neither resist or take action in a positive way. This weakness of will leaves the person unfulfilled, frustrated and feeling inadequate.

Our wills are important in enabling us to carry out those things which God has called us to do. The most common problem is weak willed attitudes which cause Christians to give in too easily when under pressure. This giving in often takes the form of blaming others or the situation. For example, 'If only I had better fellowship' or 'If only our church was not so dead' and so on. In the case of counselling we blame the client for being awkward. In all cases of weak willedness we tend to become narrow and dogmatic, resorting to theories which attempt to explain the situation away by the use of glib and trite answers. We are called by Christ to suffer with him and love even when it hurts. Only then can we know the power of his resurrection. Many never experience this because they are too weak willed to 'persevere to the end'.

Thus we can see the importance of having a sound will in working out our relationships with God and other people; this is especially so when engaged in counselling. Without it we frustrate both ourselves and the other person, causing barriers to come between us that in the end will destroy trust, that essential quality for all relationships. This weakness of will is caused by the lack of balance between the intellect and the emotions. It is therefore important to understand that the basis of a sound will is always a sound mind and sound emotions working in harmony with each other.

One of the words used for will in the Bible is 'Shabaoth'. It means the power to organize and direct all óne's forces in a positive way. It is also used of marshalling armies in battle. In the Te Deum, God is called 'The Lord God of Shabaoth' because he does this in working out his purpose in creation. As we are made in his image we need to pray that we may be given grace to marshal all our personal forces in carrying out his purpose for us within his kingdom. This is how we can strengthen our wills in a positive healthy way so that they are not weak or in disarray, but well tuned and in harmony, so that they can enable us to rise to every challenge that God sets before us.

Conscience
This is a normal awareness within us that enables us to decide between right and wrong. A good conscience will help us to be guided in our relationships, and conduct all our affairs in a positive way. A bad and unreliable conscience can get us into all sorts of difficulties and distort the way in which we respond to others. It is therefore vital that a counsellor should have a healthy and well adjusted conscience.

The problem with conscience is that it is very delicate, hard to define, but most sensitive. Like the will, it does not seem to stand on its own but is largely a product of the relationship between other aspects of ourselves and our social conditioning. In severely mentally ill people such as psychopaths it does not seem to exist, but at the other extreme in some people it is overactive and responds so falsely that it cripples them as people by creating a guilt so false that it is ridiculous. St Paul was very aware of the problem of conscience as is apparent in 1 Corinthians Chapter 4, verses 1 to 5. He sees how easy it is to have our consciences manipulated by other people. 'I shall not be judged by you or any other person' he says, 'Indeed I will not even judge myself. The only one who can judge what I do is God, therefore I continually lay my life before him in complete trust and openness, so that he can condition how my conscience works'. (My own paraphrase of what I hear Paul saying). The great divines and spiritual guides of all ages have been aware of the delicate nature of the human conscience, its importance in our relationship with God and the need to nurture it with care. For example, Matthew Henry's commentary on 1 John Chapter 3, verses 20 to 22 says:

> Verse 20. Our heart here is our self – reflecting judicial power, whereby we can take cognizance of ourselves, and accordingly pass a judgement on our state towards God; and so it is the same with conscience. Conscience is God's vice-regent, calls the court in His name and acts for Him. If conscience condemns us God does too . . . If conscience acquit us, God does so too . . . Let conscience therefore be HEARD, BE WELL INFORMED, and DILIGENTLY ATTENDED TO.

In conclusion, our conscience must be well cared for and adjusted so that it does not lead us astray by false responses. One that is too sensitive is as dangerous as one that does not respond at all. Both indicate a bad or uncultivated relationship with the true and living God. The practical exercises include a simple prayer for the correct adjustment of our conscience.

Chapter II

Practical Aspects of Our Relationship with God

External factors which are relevant in our relationship with God

We have subjectively looked at ourselves as spiritual beings considering all our component parts as they are involved in our relationship with God. We have seen how together they form a unity of personality which the Bible calls 'Nephesh' or living soul. This Biblical/Christian view of the human being does not consider the Greek/Philosophical view of people being composed of body, mind and spirit as adequate. A human being therefore from a Christian point of view is a spiritual being, wonderful and complex, magnificent and yet frail, operating as a unity, now clothed in a material body during its time on earth, but destined to be clothed in a glorified and new spiritual body in the world to come. This puts us in the position of having to relate to two worlds. The material world of the present, which is real but destined eventually to pass away, and the spiritual world which in the present we can only know in part, but which in the future will completely replace the material world. In our relationship with God we need to take proper and relevant cognizance of both, giving each the respect due to them.

This World

Because our physical bodies are the temple of the spirit we must care properly for their physical needs. If our physical bodies are sick, then we as 'living souls' do not reside at ease within them. The pain this causes can blunt our spiritual awareness. Our spiritual and physical bodies are so related to each other that not only does a sick physical body adversely affect the soul, but a sick spirit can make the physical body sick also. There are two basic indications of a bad relationship with the material world.

The first one is clinging to material things so that they hold back our full development as spiritual persons. In a counsellor who has not let go this tendency to cling to the material, death in any form will automatically be felt as being failure. By death, not only physical death is meant, but such events as a sudden end to the counselling relationship brought about by the counsellee because they no longer feel in need, or the counsellee becoming overtly worse in that their behaviour becomes more anti-social, or the emotional pain more obvious or intense. There are many more possibilities than can be mentioned here, but in general the counsellor who is clinging to material values rather than ones based on the kingdom of God will tend to evaluate their work by Hollywood style 'they lived happily ever after' success models which are so superficial that they cover up the true situation. In short, they totally fail to understand the meaning of the cross and the more deep and mysterious ways of the kingdom of God.

The second is a more certain indication that we have got it wrong and are therefore endangering the health of our relationship with God. It is, in one word, striving. The tendency to strive to be good, holy or to achieve any other idealistic goal is the most prevalent cause of a breakdown of our relationship with God. It is a true mark of worldliness. When a counsellor finds pressure coming up from within, to try harder to give more time to clients, looking at more and more new techniques that might just be the answer for this one or that one, and finally praying harder with more intense fervour, beware. This is the stage at which the material world is either rejected in favour of a magical spiritual solution, or the spiritual world rejected in favour of a falsely 'scientific' materialistic solution. Impatience is at the root of this, and impatience is a certain symptom of spiritual immaturity and an infantile relationship with God.

This tendency to strive to become good and acceptable to God is a soul destroyer and a lie. It is at the root of the worst of heresies like Pelagianism. Kierkegaard the Danish Christian thinker said 'The greatest Christian heresy is to believe that the opposite of sin is virtue. No, the opposite of sin is grace'. We need always to resist the temptation to strive to be good and to keep set rules or principles because this only brings us to guilt and despair. It lays us open to being manipulated and used by those whom we seek to help, without positive benefits for anyone. In our relationship with God we renounce this way of the world, a way which involves putting on an act by presenting our best side, and hiding our worst parts. We open ourselves to God just as we are, letting him, by the power of the Holy Spirit, work his purpose of grace in us. We are then made strong in weakness and enabled to be what God created us to become, not conditioned by the world to fit its very finite scheme of current fashion. Psalm 51, verse 6 says that God desires 'Truth in our inward parts'. A healthy relationship with him is totally dependent on our willingness to recognize and accept our worst parts, feel our weaknesses and become very frail and human in his presence.

The Spiritual World

The problem we have with the spiritual world is its vastness and our inability to know our way around it. This very frightening fact alone drives many timid and insecure people into what they see as the apparent certainty and security of materialism. The first Epistle of St John deals with this in Chapter 4. It shows how Jesus Christ is the only safe guide in this world and that satan would desire to trick us into a false sense of security even feigning gifts of the spirit by posing as an angel of light. It is because of this that so many Christian prayers end with the words 'through Jesus Christ our Lord', showing that the only certain way to God must at some point be through the mediation of Jesus. 'There is one God and one mediator between God and man . . . Christ Jesus' (1 Timothy Chapter 2 verse 5).

If we are aware of this, and of our Lord's claim to have power over all things in the spiritual world we will not fall into the traps set by the devil. We will in the first place treat the devil how he should be treated, that is, renounce him. The two extremes of foolishness in relationship to the devil are either to be afraid and over concerned, seeing him where he is not, or to deny that he exists at all. In either case this pleases him because it weakens our trust in God. Secondly, we will steer clear of all occultist practices, from horoscopes to seances, witchcraft and spiritualism. All are deceitful and will destroy our peace with God eventually. Such practices can bring about a sense of joy and release in the immediate. They can also give physical healing, but the end will be spiritual destruction. Many who have been involved with these things need expert ministry and the advice of a spiritual director should be sought.

I have found consistently over the years that this is a very difficult area in which many mistakes are made. The fault seems to be that there are not many people adequately equipped both spiritually and psychologically to perceive the true nature of those who have problems in this area. Some tend to write off completely anything demonic or of a purely spiritual nature by trying to give a psychological explanation to it. The gift of spiritual discernment is essential and this is something people either have or do not have. It is a gift of God and cannot be taught. It can be recognised and those who have it need to keep it sharpened by a sound prayer life and disciplined walk with God. Often leaders in Churches are deficient in this area, not able to recognise the gift or lack of it in others when they do not have it themselves. We are in need of simple people who are saints and church leaders with the ability to recognise, encourage and support them. Such people more than anyone else are likely to have this gift.

The other extreme of foolishness in this area is shown by those of fundamentalist and simplistic faith who spiritualise everything and do not recognise problems whose roots are purely psychological. These people, although appearing to be spiritual, are in fact totally without spiritual discernment in most cases and have a spiritual life that is largely a fantasy world in which fears are projected onto fantasy demons. In my experience when talking to such people they are so out of touch spiritually that if they came up against the real powers of evil they would be completely floored. Not only are such people spiritually out of touch, they have also lost touch with their own emotions. In view of this it is my opinion that anyone involved in spiritual direction should be competent both spiritually and psychologically as well as being an experienced and mature person. It does, however encourage me that most ordinary people seem to have a gut feeling about whom they can trust in these matters. It is the over sophisticated and power seeking person who is most easily deceived.

Thirdly, be very suspicious of all religion and outward piety. It is not rituals that lead us to God, but repentance and belief in the Gospel. Some of the most evil and deceitful people in the world have been religious. Religion is a subtle form of inverted worldliness aimed at making people feel good by shutting God out. The only valid place for any ritual in a Christian's life is as an expression of an inner spiritual grace. It comes as a spontaneous act from the soul of the truly godly, but cannot be taught or drilled into people without great risk of cutting them off from the living God.

From a purely Christian point of view based upon what we read of Jesus Christ in the four Gospels the problem of religion as opposed to faith is evident. Mankind is biased towards being 'religious'. It is a natural instinct towards our need of God and the supernatural. This instinct however can lead into danger, the main one being that it becomes mixed in with the lust for power and also the avoidance of pain. True faith involves the opposite, namely a denial of our lust for power and an acceptance of pain, which means that we wrestle with it and seek grace to overcome it in whatever form we may experience it. The whole of Jesus Christ's life declares this. He refused worldly power and status. He wrestled with pain and the forces of darkness in the Garden of Gethsemane. He was falsely accused and condemned by the religious leaders of the day. He died a cruel death, overcame and rose from the dead. One of the oldest of Christian statements of faith proclaims this . . . Christ has died, Christ is risen, Christ will come again.

In His teaching we are continually warned of this danger. May I just refer to a few of the many of His parables and statements on this subject. They provide good material for meditation.

(i) *St Matthew's Gospel Chapter 23*

This is called the seven woes to the Pharisees. In it Jesus lists the ways in which religious people not only cut themselves off from God, but how they also destroy the faith of others and ruin their lives. I find this a very salutary warning and it seems to me to be one many spiritual leaders never seem to learn.

(ii) *St Matthew's Gospel Chapter 15 verses 1 to 9*

This passage is particularly interesting for two reasons. Firstly it shows how the religious leaders of the time had fallen into the religious trap of rigidly following their man made traditions, and, secondly, Jesus quotes Isaiah the Old Testament Prophet showing that he was in the Prophetic tradition himself, which had always been aware of this problem. It seems that the same applies today. Negative religiosity is a flaw in human nature and will always be with us. It is simply just another aspect of sin. For further Old Testament evidence on this point it would be worth reading Amos Chapter 7. In this book it is religious practice that is seen as Israel's sin.

(iii) In conclusion may I suggest the following parables of Jesus that support this theme in His teaching.

Matthew Chapter 25 verses 31 to the end . . . The Last Judgement.

Luke Chapter 10 verses 29 to 37 . . . The Good Samaritan.

Luke Chapter 18 verses 9 to 14 . . . The prayers of the Pharisee and the Tax Collector.

The main point Jesus is making in these three stories is that it is not the religious person who gets it right. It is therefore very important to be aware of the pitfalls of being 'religious'.

Finally, after the first three points, the reader might feel completely defeated, throw up their hands in despair and say, 'Who then can be saved!!' Such a response is more positive than at first sight it would appear because it contains within it an essential prerequisite for a sound relationship with God. This is true humility, and needs to be distinguished from the negative and false humility, of which there is too much around.

False humility can easily be programmed into people by religious social conditioning. It is of the kind that makes people feel so utterly useless and negative that they are afraid to do anything, even trust God. Such people do not believe that they can ever be anything other than someone who just believes what those in authority say and will avoid all responsibility, especially for acknowledging their own feelings. The answer they give when asked to care for another person in need is, 'That is best left to those who know'. Real humility comes from those who have sufficient awareness to see how complex and impossible many situations in life can be, but at the same time believe that if they can trust God in such situations, he by his grace can create something positive even in the most hopeless cases. This humility puts a person in a positively trusting relationship with God, because such people have both seen the truth and made an honest response to it. They are in a position to 'let go and let God' which makes them available as a counsellor in a way that those who only depend on themselves cannot be. Nobody can become this kind of person, humble and trusting towards God, at a stroke. They essentially have to grow slowly and surely over a period of time.

Spiritual Growth

Physical growth is something we all take for granted, but there is a definite tendency towards believing that once a person has become a Christian, they have arrived, and all Christians are at the same level of understanding and spiritual strength. Spiritual growing pains and agonies are very much part of learning to mature in faith and trust in God, as are the pains and agonies associated with physical growth and development. St Paul, in 1 Corinthians 13, points this out and so does St Peter in his first Epistle Chapter 2. The new Christian is like a baby and cannot be expected to understand or cope with situations in the same way that one who has been a long time in the faith can. This is a very important truth which, if ignored, can cause tensions between Christians in fellowship. We need to be aware of this so that we do not use other people as a yardstick by which to measure our own spiritual stature, but seek to love and serve on the level we are at, trusting in God, by the power of the Holy Spirit, to lead us on. The skill of pastoral care and spiritual direction lies in knowing where people are in their spiritual growth, and then directing them to the right food and stimulus. It is impossible to develop this skill unless we ourselves are aware of our own spiritual growth rate with reasonable accuracy, and are also committed enough to do what is necessary to feed ourselves in a relevant way, enabling growth in God's time scale. It is therefore so important for those who have a ministry of counselling to also have supervision and spiritual direction themselves, for the sake of their own spiritual growth as much as for the benefit of those whom they seek to help.

There is one very important difference between physical and spiritual growth, and we must take note of it. It is that in physical growth there is always a point at which a peak is reached and then decline leading to death sets in. In spiritual growth, once we begin, it is a steady process of growing stronger and stronger. Death is an end that comes only when one ceases to be fed. Only spiritual starvation can cause spiritual death, and then it needs to be complete starvation. Whereas physical growth has a natural end in this world's scheme of things, spiritual growth knows no end in this world and its true completion is in the next. Much more could be said about spiritual growth, but the following four points are very valuable indicators of how we are growing in our relationship with God. They are:

(i) An increasing ability to accept the previously unacceptable in ourselves, and to accept other people as they are, warts and all.

(ii) An increase in patience which enables us to endure cheerfully the sufferings of this world, especially when we feel misunderstood and badly treated. Together with this goes an ability to see the funny side of our own tragedies.

(iii)A growing tendency not to take the things of this world too seriously but to see them as the transient things they are. This puts us in a position to truly enjoy the good things of this world because we do not invest much hope in them. While they last we enjoy them, when they pass away we can let them go and be replaced by the next thing without mourning their loss. We can do this because our citizenship is indeed in heaven and we are moving onto something better all the time, even in death.

(iv)A real sense of joy just to be in God's presence at any place and at any time. We can become so satisfied with this presence that nothing else is of any importance. This sets us free from the concern about what other people think of us and it also has the effect of improving our relationships with others, because we have less need to live our lives through them. When we do not need others for our wellbeing because God has become our strength and stay, we are less likely to use them and more likely to love them.

People have many facets to their personalities, some of which remain hidden until an appropriate stage in their spiritual growth is reached. Then these hidden things are revealed, but not always understood. It is within the context of relationships, both with God and with other people, that growth which comes of gaining understanding as these hidden facets become known to us, takes place. We dare not use our relationship with those we counsel just as a means of promoting our own growth. It is inevitable that this happens to some degree, but we must be aware enough of it not to let it adversely affect these people. This can be safeguarded by having a commitment to working continually on our relationship with God in the context of fellowship with other Christians who are at least our peers in these things.

Finally it must be emphasised that a relationship is something to be lived out and not merely theorized about. When there is a commitment to the working out part, then insight and understanding can eventually come. In view of this let us turn our attention to the practical working out of this key relationship, that of the counsellor with God, setting it within the context of the whole network of human relationships in which it would normally take place.

Practical Exercises

All these exercises are very individual. They are to be practised alone. This does not mean that our relationship with God is just an individual matter because it is not. We have to be in right relationship with God and with other people. We will have a different relationship with fellow Christians from that which we have with those who are not Christians but both relationships are important, not only for the other people, but also for ourselves, for God and for his kingdom. All relationships are inter-related but the key one, the cornerstone of all others is our relationship with God. The following exercises are aimed at helping this one to develop, but in so doing all other relationships are taken into account.

(i) Learning to be still   People who cannot be still and at peace with themselves are sick spiritually. Eventually they will become ill physically. The exercise of learning to sit still in God's presence is a very basic one and needs to be learnt first. It is simple in theory; all one has to do is to sit still every day for as long as it is possible. Begin by doing so for about twenty minutes, then extend it as the need arises or as the desire grows. Allow all feelings to surface and thoughts to wander until a situation of quiet is reached. For some people this could take a year or so of practice, but the will to persevere until the peace is reached is the only way to do it. Feelings that come up in a persistent way can be talked over with a counsellor, but in general it is better to sit them out until they subside.

It is helpful, but not essential to keep repeating a verse of scripture such as 'Be still and know that I am God' or just to say the word 'Jesus' over and over as a means of stilling the mind. Those who have a good imagination can picture Jesus in their mind as a way of stilling it. Until a good mastery of this exercise has been reached, the ones following will not be of much help.

(ii) Allowing God to ease out our tensions   This is an extension of the previous exercise. Even those who are right with God and at peace within themselves pick up the stresses and tensions of the world in which we have to live. We must avoid the barrenness that comes from a busy life and the corresponding temptation to fit God into a corner that is convenient. Our time with God and reference to him must become the basis of everything we do. When we are under some particular pressure, feel overwhelmed or just do not know how to get everything done, the worst thing we can do is to try harder or to increase our working time. This is futile, for its only achievement is to wear us out.

What we should do is to drop everything as soon as is convenient, go to a quiet place and allow God to 'love us better' by easing out our tensions and renewing us with energy. We then return to our task with a new outlook, enabled to focus specifically on what is troubling us. We feel the tension in whatever part of our body it is focused, or we allow an emotion related to the problem, eg fear, anger or frustration, to come right up into the mind and then ooze out to God. We should be prepared to take whatever time is necessary for our peace and energy to be restored. When we have really mastered the first exercise and are disciplined in the time we spend with God this exercise is an emergency one and does not take too long.

(iii) Silent worship and adoration   Just sit still, close the eyes, let the imagination picture Jesus and in silence praise and adore him as one would another person who is loved deeply. This simple exercise done from time to time can lead to spontaneous praise and adoration that can become sung or spoken. When we get to this stage some good experience of the creation or another person can strike off within us chords of uplifting praise to God. It can lead us to see the glory and wonders of creation. All colours become more vivid and intense, even people can seem more beautiful in form and character. We can also experience the presence of the Godhead because Jesus, in human form, is not only the way to God but also a window through which we can glimpse God's glory. This exercise is one to be approached in a relaxed way after No (i) has been mastered. It depends on us being able to allow the Holy Spirit to have his way.

(iv) When someone annoys or disturbs us   This happens very frequently in every day life. All of us know people with whom we feel embarrassed or uncomfortable as well as those who just annoy or make us angry. This happens not just by the things they say, but sometimes by what they are and we can't always put our finger on the cause of the trouble. Our natural response is either to argue or get angry as an attempt to defend ourselves, or just to avoid these difficult people because they are not our types. None of these reactions are the right way to deal with such situations if we are to develop our relationships with God and other people. We must look more deeply into the nature of what is going on inside ourselves, in the relationship between us and the other person, and where God comes into the situation.

The first thing to do in such a situation is to stand back from it and allow God the Holy Spirit to work and reveal the truth to us. Sometimes we are left in the dark because it is not yet God's time. If this is so we must wait patiently and go on living with the situation, putting it regularly into God's hands until something happens to open it up. At other times we may be made aware that the problem is in us. God does use others to reflect back to us our own inadequacies. When this is the case we must prayerfully attend to what has been shown to us, leaving out the other person except for thanking God that he has so used them to bless us. The third possibility is that the problem is in the other person and something in us has made them aware of it, in which case we just hold them up to God for him to work his way in them. We must be very wary of approaching the other person in any way because by so doing we could be holding up God's work in them. More will be said about this in the next exercise.

The best way to carry out what has been described is by use of the imagination. Sit quietly and in the imagination relive the incident that upset you, or picture the person who makes you feel uncomfortable in a familiar situation, with yourself present. When the picture is in the mind, pray first for yourself, that God will show you what is going on in you, and then for the other person, and finally for enlightenment as to what God would like to show you of the situation.

When we do this it is likely that one of three things may happen. The first one is that we just go blank in our minds and enter a situation of peace. When this is the case, do no more, for as far as we are concerned the case is closed and it is in God's hands. The second one is that we become aware of strong feelings within us. Let these feelings have full expression to God. Sometimes they will be nothing to do with the person who stirred them up and so we leave that person out and seek to deal with our own feelings. We may or may not need counselling for this, but we must seek God's help in deciding for ourselves. The third possibility is that we will be given a concern for the other person and sometimes considerable insight into their situation. If this is so, make them someone for whom to pray regularly and see where this leads. In some cases it will stay at the prayer level, and in others all kinds of developments can take place in our relationship with that person.

(v) Repairing relationships   This is a very important subject for the Christian because we are commanded to love everyone and good relationships are of the essence of the faith. Loving our enemies and those who persecute us cannot be avoided. The golden rule is that we never rush in and by our own efforts seek to put those relationships right. We must accept that this is beyond us, and by use of the imagination turn to prayer.

The method is to place the other person in the mind and just hold them up to God for several minutes. Say nothing other than words like 'God, this is your son/daughter, you know what is going on between us, I therefore seek your help in this situation for which I am not adequate. Help me to love them as you loved your enemies'. This might be all we can do for ages, even years. If it is, we must be content with this. Often, however, things change in our relationship slowly, but certainly in ways we cannot understand. In some cases we are shown, either by God putting a desire in our heart or by external events that just happen, ways to repair the relationship. Two important final words on this subject, firstly be slow to take action, and secondly, the state of our relationships with others is a direct indicator of our relationship with God. Take this issue very seriously.

(vi) Using our dreams   In the Bible dreams were important in the lives of God's people. They still are today but we have neglected this area of experience to our own great impoverishment. We should view all our dreams as an internal extension of our external experiences. They always relate to the whole of our lives, both chronologically in terms of our personal history, and also culturally in terms of where our life has its setting within the context of the whole of humanity. As well as this broader background they also relate to all those day to day things that disturb or stimulate us emotionally as we live out our lives each day. Therefore, we must never draw a firm line between our dream world and the rest of our life as lived in the external world. They are in fact one whole and we need to integrate them, not separate them from the day to day affairs of life.

Sometimes God reveals things direct to people by the way of dreams. An example of this in the Bible is how it was revealed to the wise men in a dream that Herod was not to be trusted, (Matthew Chapter 2 verse 12). I have experienced this myself and know many other people who have the same experience when having to respond to difficult situations. The experience of the wise men is often repeated in the Bible and in the experience of those throughout the ages who have lived the life of faith. It is important, therefore, to share our dreams in fellowship with other Christians so that we can test them and come to a good understanding of what God might be saying before taking any action.

Some important things to be aware of in our dreams:

(i) Recurring themes or patterns which when examined can uncover deep areas of fear, doubt and insecurity. These things often make us over active to compensate for a lack of trust in God's love for us. This in turn leads to our efforts continually failing or falling short of expectations, mainly because we have an unrealistic view of ourselves and what God expects of us. As a result tensions and frustration are built up within us over a period of time. Because this build up is slow, it tends to go unnoticed for a very long time and in many cases cause very serious and deeply rooted spiritual problems.

(ii) The images and scenarios of our dreams are always a mixture of the bizarre and ordinary, the obvious and mystifying, the congruent and incongruent. Why is this? In short I think it is because our dreams connect us up with the depths of our unconscious mind and at times the spiritual world that is beyond us as an individual person. In making this connection it does not abandon our here and now day to day experiences of ordinary life in this world. This accounts for the strange and often incoherent mixture. Dreams are about a wider reality that has more wholeness than a purely material view of our existence, and as such they are not easily understood. In view of this I believe they should be pondered over and prayed about as well as shared with a good spiritual director. It may take time to understand them, and some aspects may never be understood or even need to be. A life of prayer guided by the Holy Spirit will give us wisdom in this. I also think that whereas theories about dreams such as Jung's idea of archetypal images have their place and use, they can be dangerous as far as interpretation is concerned because they tend to impose restricting intellectual concepts on a dream, that could mask the true meaning that it is trying to express. I would say that I would favour the common sense hands on approach to understanding dreams as opposed to the methods that use rigidly imposed methods based upon psychological schools of thought that are claimed to have a 'scientific' basis.

(iii) It is always important to distinguish between dreams that take place in deep sleep, which are the more significant ones, and those which are just a continuation of the days unresolved bits of business as we drop off to sleep. The relevance of this type is largely that it indicates anxiety about our daily business for some reason or other.

(iv) Some dreams are important in the healing process. These are called 'Abreactive Dreams'. They are best described as a reliving of past hurts and traumatic experiences so that they can be 'worked out of our system'. Sometimes people need to talk these through and pray about them in other instances they just happen and seem to be self healing. The other important aspect of this kind of dream is where the experience has been repressed and the pain surrounding it is showing itself in negative behaviour patters or psychosomatic illness. I have found that prayer on the basis of Psalm 139, that is usually silent and just asking that the Holy Spirit might lead the client into the truth about their problem, can lead to abreactive dreams. One needs to be careful in the interpretation of these because they often are composed of symbolism that is not the same as the incident that caused the trauma originally. This relates to what has been called 'false memory syndrome' in cases of child abuse that has been denied for years. The person concerned may well have been abused, misunderstood or unloved, but not in precisely the same way that the dream indicates.

(v) In middle age, ie from about forty to seventy years, many people have 'Recapitulative Dreams'. These are dreams in which childhood and early adulthood parts of their life is relived in dreams. These can be sad or happy dreams and they are part of a process of spiritual and emotional growth which must be taken seriously if we are to grow into a happy and fulfilled old age. It is about putting our life together as a meaningful whole, a process of integration. Therefore they must not be ignored, but looked at, understood and in some case action taken. I have found in my own life that deeper faith develops when these dreams are taken seriously and treated with the same value as all that is happening from day to day in our lives. They often help us to understand the meaning of what is happening to us in the present and are an important factor to be considered in spiritual direction.

(vi) Prophetic dreams, when God speaks to an individual, are quite rare in my experience, but their impact is such that one knows they are in a different category. I have had several myself and know a number of people who have also had them. Like all prophecy they do need rigorous testing. We should also be slow to jump to conclusions because by holding back and giving events a chance to verify the content of the dream, my experience is that sooner or later any really genuine one is verified. One thing we must always do is to pray about what we have been shown as though it had happened. This gives the intiative to God and prevents us taking precipitous or foolish action. Most of these dreams relate to things that are relevant to the life of the person who dreams them, but from time to time people do have such dreams that relate to wider events.

(vii) In a culture where materialism predominates and dreams are seen as being the result of eating too much cheese before going to bed, most people repress their dreams. This does not mean that they do not dream, it means that the dreams are not registered in definite visual images. It is my experience in counselling and spiritual direction that with such people the process of counselling and prayer breaks the repressive barriers and brings to life the imagery of dreams. It is usually after a few sessions in which there has been prayer that the Holy Spirit gives the client an inner awareness of the truth about themselves, and they begin to register their dreams. Often this begins with vague images in black and white or two tone grey. From this a development takes place until the dreams are in bright technicolour. It is my opinion that those who are healthily in touch with their inner selves will always dream in bright technicolour and those who are not cannot.

(viii) Finally, often poeple have dreams that are incomplete. They wake up and the story of the dream has not come to a conclusion. In such cases it is valuable to be able to continue them by sitting in a relaxed way, with eyes closed, and pray that God will give the grace to run them on from where they ended. This often happens quite easily if we are able to relax enough. Our dream world is of the same ilk as our fantasy world, the only difference being that dreams happen when we are asleep and therefore we have much less control, so that we cannot put a halt to them. When waking we have to will our fantasy world into action and that is why our dream was incomplete. Upon waking we simply took control and stopped it, therefore an act of will to allow it to continue will always work if we so desire. We do not make the incomplete dream continue, we allow it to do so because in fact it has a life of its own.

(vii) Training our conscience This is important because it is so easily manipulated by other people, especially distressed ones who come for help. We should seek so to train, that the Holy Spirit is its principle guide. The following prayer is suggested as a guideline for this:

> Heavenly Father, please help me to train my conscience through the working of your Holy Spirit so that it is free from all morbid fears, trivial responses and the unjust accusations of others. Give me a conscience that approves what you approve and condemns what you would condemn, for Jesus Christ's sake and the building of your kingdom. Amen.

Pray such a prayer regularly when people or situations arise that raise feelings of guilt, be patient and slow in response, subjecting the whole situation carefully in prayer to God along these lines.

(viii) Strengthening the will In order to have our wills made strong we must firstly be open with God in prayer about everything. Secondly, having come to this point of openness with honesty, we need to align our will with God's will. This will involve us in wrestling prayer similar to that which our Lord prayed in the Garden of Gethsemane (see Luke Chapter 22 verses 39-46). This kind of disputing with God must be worked out right to its conclusion, no matter how long it takes. It may even be necessary to set a day aside for prayer and fasting so that we can get into the wrestle as our Lord did in the wilderness (see Luke Chapter 4 verses 1-14). One of the main purposes of fasting is to strengthen the will, but it must be done with care, for a specific purpose, and under the guidance of the Holy Spirit. Again, we need to consult a spiritual director in this matter.

A weak willed counsellor will too easily acquiesce into making things easy for a counsellee struggling over matters of will. In situations where it is sensed that a battle of wills is taking place, usually during a long period of silence, the counsellor should pray silently for God's grace to enable the counsellee's will to hold out until the Holy Spirit can reveal the truth of the situation to them. It is always disastrous in the long run when a weak willed counsellor is pressed into letting a client off the hook by giving less than adequate but immediately pleasing responses. Martin Israel writes:

> God alone knows the answer to every human question for he sees each creature in its final completion, an end of growth contributed to equally by divine grace and the patient development of the will of the person struggling towards integrity of purpose and fulfilment of design. (Spirit of Counsel p62).

Anyone who is going to be able to help others to fulfilment in Christ must have the will to stay with the other person's pain as they struggle, and not opt out or seek glib answers. This involves them having a very strong will, which in turn only comes by conflict and wrestling prayer of the Gethsemane type. We must be prepared to 'sweat it out with Christ' even if it involves sleepless nights for a while. Exercises (i), (ii), (iii) and (iv) provide the framework for doing this. Fasting can be used in addition when necessary. May I conclude with a verse of scripture suitable for the basis of a will strengthening meditation:

> But those who wait for the Lord shall renew their strength,
> they shall mount up with wings as eagles,
> they shall run and not be weary,
> they shall walk and not faint.
>
> (Isaiah Chapter 40 verse 31)

Our will to do God's will can only be strengthened by waiting on him and receiving the Holy Spirit. We will only be able to have a strong, healthy and well aligned will if we are in a state of emotional harmony within. Therefore mastery of exercises (i) to (iv) is a vital part of will strengthening because a healthy will is not an entity in itself. It develops out of our interactions with other people, God, and the everyday events of life. These events must include hardship and suffering as well as joy and encouragement. The hardships must be faced and wrestled with by the grace of God, and not avoided, because they are part of the whole pattern and purpose of God.

(vi) Receiving God's guidance   This is a very important issue for two reasons. Firstly it is a necessity if we are to give real spiritual help to people, because we will find ourselves operating in areas too difficult for human wisdom alone, with people who have exhausted all human resources. Secondly, it is only too easy to mistake the voice of God for our own imagination. What therefore is the most important resource a Christian counsellor has, also happens to be the most open to abuse and misunderstanding. It is important to look at guidance within a sound theological framework to be sure that we get it right. This needs to be emphasised, because we can only understand the practical importance of such a theoretical structure when we relate a doctrine such as that of the transcendent and immanent nature of God to the practicalities of divine guidance. This doctrine states that God is at the same time both within us, his creation, and outside us. His Spirit is at work within the whole of creation, working a common purpose towards the building up of his kingdom. Therefore we must expect to hear his voice both within the depths of our own soul, and also in the world outside ourselves. The whole testimony of scripture and the history of the faith points this out so clearly. Now, in actual practice, where do we begin?

The best starting point is within ourselves. Pray daily that in all things the Holy Spirit will give the gifts of wisdom and discernment. These are the most important of all the gifts because they give us the grace not only to hear God speaking to us from within by means of dreams, visions, or putting words into our mouths at crucial times, but they also increase our awareness of what God is doing in the world around us. Guidance that is reliable always has an inner witness of peace and certainty that accords with the external realities of the current situation what ever it might be.

The next step is awareness of the external situation in which we find ourselves. The simple theological statement 'Jesus is Lord' means that God has put him in charge of all history. Therefore everything that happens is a step towards the end when he will put everything right. Because of this, even things we do not like personally are parts of a greater purpose. We do not need to understand it all, only our place within it. Therefore only expect to be guided in those things that are God's concern for you. The general spiritual busybody who is into everything is not God's servant, but one who can easily become a victim of self-deceit. Beware of this (see John Chapter 21 verses 20-23).

It is also important to test cautiously our inner awareness of God's voice. The person who goes around telling others that the Lord has told them something, but has no awareness of outside factors, or who will not allow the message to be tested, is always one who is not to be trusted. There is an exception to this rule, such as the times when in a tight corner that we say things before we have time to think about them, and surprise ourselves at what has been said. In these instances one is aware that someone else has spoken the words, and that as the speaker one is just listening to them. They are also very relevant to the immediate situation bringing to light more than we could imagine possible. These comparatively rare happenings are a result of prayer for wisdom and discernment. We should rejoice in them because they humble us and glorify the mercy, power and grace of God at work in those who are truly his.

In all other cases of feeling God has shown us something, we should either share what we think has been told us with other Christians, or allow events either to prove or disprove their validity. God will at times use non-believers to confirm or deny the reality of what he is trying to show us, so we must be patient and allow things to work out. An important part of patience is giving ourselves time to stand back from the situation in which we are seeking guidance, reflect upon it prayerfully and just see the way things are going without manipulating them.

The things within ourselves that block out guidance are: pride, anxiety, dogma that puts God into a little box of our own making, an urge to manipulate things for our own ends believing that we are helping God, and finally, failure to have a disciplined life based on prayer. Lack of commitment to practising the previous exercise will make this discourse on guidance irrelevant.

(x) Discipline and rule of life   This is the basis of all the previous exercises since it is the means by which we find the time to practise them. A good relationship can only be built up with another person if time is found to spend with them. So it is with God, and just as many husbands become strangers to their wives through the pressure of doing work that is not really necessary, so do many believers become strangers to God by working too hard for him. In both cases the end is disaster, the breakdown of the relationship. A rule of life that ensures that we have time to be with God and do these exercises that develop the relationship. If we don't have time for this we deny Christ and are unable to work for him at all. Time spent with God ends by putting us in the right situation and frame of mind to work effectively for him and not get in his way.

It is a good thing to make our own rule of life by discussing it with another more mature Christian or spiritual director. It must be flexible and related to our present situation. It must make time to spend with God and also time relaxing with other people and pursuing some kind of hobby. These three things contribute to making us rounded people and are a counterbalance against being workaholic and narrow. It is important to commit ourselves to some task for Christ and to consider how we manage our money so that contributions are made to the support of his work. The rule needs to be revised under the guidance of a spiritual director as life goes on and circumstances change. It must never become an unbreakable rule like that of the Medes and the Persians, but a reliable guideline within which we are constantly reminded of the essentials of the Christian way of life.

Another dimension of a sound rule is that it must be within the structures of the Church as they are rooted in the Gospel. Jesus said: 'If you love me, you will keep my commandments'. One commandment he gave was: 'Do this in remembrance of me' and 'Unless you eat my flesh and drink my blood you shall have no life within you'. This means regularly receiving Holy Communion. He also said: 'This is my commandment, that you love one another as I have loved you'. Only active participation in the life of the local Church will enable us to fulfil this one. There is also the need to pray with small groups of Christians as well as worshipping in a larger congregation.

Finally, we must learn to love our enemies and do good to those who hate us. These people will sometimes be in the local Churches as well as in the outside world. Exercises (iv) and (v) will help us in doing this. The important thing is that we should stay with situations in which we meet such people as much for our own benefit as theirs.

In conclusion, the purpose of this short overview is to offer practical guidance to Christians who are doing any kind of counselling, but also basing it on a theoretical structure, to enable the avoidance of superficial and misguided counselling which can so easily happen. Some may find these guidelines enough, others may wish to ditch them and carry on in their own established way. God bless you both!!! For those who wish to take it further I have included a list of suggested further reading which may be found at the end of the book. Keep at it, the only limits are those to which the Holy Spirit leads you.

Part Two

The Counsellor and the Family

Chapter III

Individual Personality and its Development

INTRODUCTION
This section is not intended to be a counselling manual with techniques for solving family problems or providing all the answers. This would be impossible to write, not only because of the complexities of families, but also of the society in which they are set, and of the nature of human personality which is the essence of being.

There are two basic assumptions behind what is written here. The first one is that being human is a very important issue and to be fully human is something everyone has to grow into. We are born with much potential, but it has to be developed. In the process of development our relationships with other people play a vital part. These relationships take place all our life and in the context of different groups, but the key group that is most formative is the basic nuclear family; mum, dad, and children.

The second assumption is that of a Christian morality. As one formed in the Christian tradition and still a part of it, I am bound to write from that basic standpoint. This tradition is a very wide and all embracing one, not essentially governed by lots of rules and regulations, but by the spirit of love – of God, neighbour and oneself. Iranaeus, the second century Bishop of Lyon sums up much of this in the words, 'The Glory of God is a human being, fully human, fully alive'. This message is my main motivation for writing; too often our churches and our cultures fail to capture the personal 'life more abundant' of which the New Testament speaks. This 'life more abundant' involves having relationships of a good quality, and the skills required for this are best gained in childhood within the context of the family.

Family life is very complex. Being in a family can be both a supportive and a destructive experience. It involves experiencing a wide variety of emotions, pleasant and unpleasant, that leave their mark on our characters. An understanding of this is important because sometimes a situation that feels bad when it happens, may in the long term be good if viewed in its fullest context, rather than just the immediate effect it has on the individual. The same can be true in reverse. For example, a child who grew up in a loving family, but in very restricted material circumstances, could well find the early years of life a frustrating struggle, but as a result mature into a very competent person, able to manage business affairs and life generally very well. On the other hand another person whose family were equally loving and caring but were very affluent, could as a result grow into an adult unable to cope and manage at all, always in debt no matter how much money was available, and in a permanent state of non-coping. I have on several occasions come across these two extremes within one family, the first child having been born before the war, in the 1930s when money was short, and the second born after the war in the late 1940s when money was more plentiful. For our personal growth into maturity it would seem that we do not only need love as a basis, but also some adversity with which to wrestle.

If we consider the family as a social group within society, we will find it easier to distinguish between traumas which are growing points and those which are negative because they do not promote individual growth towards maturity. This, it is hoped, will provide those who are involved as helpers with family problems, with a map to guide them through perplexity.

The limits of professionalism

The professional person is one who is trained and disciplined in a particular skill. This results in their being highly competent in a limited area, and also gives them responsibilities towards the professional body that trained and authorised them. This is both good and bad. It is good in that it creates a high degree of competence and responsibility within a narrow field. It is bad in that it can create a kind of professional paranoia that has a dehumanising effect upon the professional person, an inevitable consequence of professionalism which is not often recognised or accepted.

In practice it is a defence against getting hurt, and works out something like this; because of the demands made upon the professional person by the body that trains him or her, that person believes that in the certain area where they have a very great competence, they ought to be recognised by all. This is fair enough but it can so easily put the professional person in a god-like, rather than human, relationship with those that he or she seeks to serve. Thus, if the client or patient is not responding to the professional person's method of treatment, it can become a threat to the wellbeing of the professional person. Without realising it, this threat can raise strong feelings of a paranoid kind within the professional. ('I'm being got at and undermined by this client'). The professional has either to admit to the patient or client, his or her inadequacy which could seem like a denial of the validity of their training, and a criticism of the professional body which trained and recognised them; or, on the other hand, reject the client as being unsuitable for the treatment offered, unresponsive to it, or totally beyond the pale. It is the second option that is usually taken because the pressure upon professional people from their clients and patients is such that for their own survival they have to do so.

One purpose of this book is to mobilise the non-professional sources in such a way that they can work in harmony with, and give support to, the professional by understanding and accepting the nature of both.

Counselling: professional and non-professional
All that has been said about professionalism is true of counselling, especially with the growth of professionalism in this field and the formation in recent years of the British Association for Counselling. Before we go on, it is important to say what we mean by counselling as it covers such a wide area. The British Association for Counselling has stated that:

People become engaged in counselling when a person, occupying regularly or temporarily the role of counsellor, agrees to offer time, attention and respect to another person or persons temporarily in the role of client. The task of counselling is to give the client an opportunity to explore, discover and clarify ways of living more

41

resourcefully and towards greater well-being (BAC Standards and Ethics Committee, 1979)

This definition describes what is meant whenever the word 'counselling' is used in this book. Of itself it does not equate counselling with professionalism. A balanced, warm and competent person can offer counselling to another, as described by the BAC definition, in a way that is equally as valid as that offered by a professional counsellor. What then is the difference between professional and non-professional counselling?

There are a number of important differences, to do with situation and availability, relevance, general guidance and dealing with specific problems in depth. However, the basic skills required in good counselling are common to both professional and non-professional alike.

In terms of contrasts we may note that:

(i)   The professional counsellor always works in a formal way with set hours of work and appointments. He or she is paid to do this work, either by an agency or some fee paying system. The non-professional is more informal. Their counselling takes place in a wide variety of situations, such as a chat over coffee in the kitchen, a talk in the pub, on the train or a walk. Money is not paid for these informal sessions and if appointments are made, they are usually flexible.

(ii)   The professional usually works at a great depth and in a more specialised way. They are disciplined by a school of counselling and tend to specialise – eg marriage, family problems, vocational, psycho-sexual, spiritual – so that they can cope without sacrificing skills and standards of work. Non-professionals, however, work more generally. They tend to be at the grass roots of human need, and are a kind of first-aider who comes into contact with problems at an early stage. Very few people go direct to professional counsellors. They usually come via non-professionals and often continue to be supported by them when undergoing more in-depth and specific counselling by professionals.

(iii)   The non-professional is more immediately available than the professional. This is because of the demands made on professional counsellors. Working deeply with a client can be exhausting and demanding of concentration and emotional commitment. Professionals are not free to answer a telephone at any time of the day, or drop everything to respond to a crisis. Neither can they spend a long time with a client just in supportive friendly chat. To do this would destroy the effectiveness of what they have to offer.

Thus we see the mutuality of professional and non-professional counselling. Most of this section is directed towards non-professional counsellors, but still bearing in mind the role of the professional. Later, when looking at both individual and group problems, a distinction will be made between those needing professional help, and those for whom non-professional help may well be sufficient.

When to intervene and when not to intervene
Most people who are actively involved in any of the helping professions soon become aware of two conflicting factors. There is, on the one hand, the quite amazing ability, innate in many people, to discover their own means of help and work through quite difficult situations on their own, and on the other, the most incredible blind spots and inability to do anything on their own that otherwise able people may have. Indeed, these two extremes can exist together in the same person and manifest themselves in different situations.

The helper needs to be aware of these complexities, be flexible enough to respond appropriately to each situation and to know when to intervene and when to leave alone. Often just a listening ear without comment or action is all that is required, but there will be situations where the right word or action, well timed, can unlock an emotional log jam, and enable a healing process to take place. Effective helpers are available in the right way at the right time to take the right action (which may be simply being there) in any situation where help is required. What equips such a person? In a word, understanding. This section is aimed at giving anyone who is concerned about families an understanding of what makes them tick and how important they are for us all, because this is the only sound basis from which real help can be given in times of difficulty. But before we look at families specifically we need to understand something about individual human development.

INDIVIDUAL PERSONALITY AND ITS DEVELOPMENT

Since the family is being viewed here as the basic nurture group within which the individual can grow into becoming a balanced and mature human being, we need to start with a description of the individual person. This raises two interconnected and related questions about the essential nature of a human being, and about becoming a human being.

Being human

What is a human being? . . .This is a difficult question to answer. If we take a strictly scientific view, then a human being can be seen as essentially an animal, more developed than other animals. This reduction of man to that which is measurable leaves much unaccounted for. The history of art, education and politics as well as cross-cultural experience point us to something beyond what is obviously present to a scientific observer, eg: John Smith, aged 32, height 1.8m, weight 80 kg, eye colour blue, hair colour fair, etc. It points us to a complicated mystery, to a being that not only is, but is becoming something far beyond that which now is. John Smith might be anxious about his career, have a bad relationship with his father, have phobias about spiders, be exploring religion and very into Bach or wine appreciation or fishing. All this tells us something about what is inside the psyche of John Smith that cannot be measured scientifically but has much more importance as far as his happiness is concerned, and consequently, how easy or difficult a person he is to live with.

The questions raised when this aspect of man's nature is taken into account are a mixture of the psychological, spiritual and philosophical. They are well expressed by Robert Burns at the end of his poem 'To a mouse, on turning her up in her nest with a plough, November 1785':

> But mouse, thou art not all alone,
> In proving foresight may be vain
> The best laid schemes of mice and men
> > Go oft astray
> And leave us nought but grief and pain
> > For promised joy.

> Still thou art blest compared with me
> The present only touches thee
> But oh! I backward cast my eye
> > On prospects drear
> And forward though I cannot see
> > I guess and fear.

They do not however end here with an awareness of the pain that exists in human beings in a way which the animal world does not seem to share. They go on into a philosophical and religious question of the type raised in Psalm 8, verses 5-9:

> . . . what is man that you should keep him in mind,
> mortal man that you should care for him?

> Yet you have made him little less than a god;
> with glory and honour you crowned him
> gave him power over all the works of your hand
> put all things under his feet.

(Taken from The Psalms: A New Translation, Fontana/Collins 1985)

The questionings of adult human beings which the above quotations illustrate are continually being expressed in art, religion and philosophy, showing that human beings, even though they have reached their full physical stature, seem to be always in the process of becoming rather than having arrived. The questions are continually here but the answers are not so permanent; they change with the individual's situation. This is an important factor to be taken account of in any description of human personality. It is also essential for practical purposes to be aware of those parts of the human personality that are always there, through whose agency we become what we are destined to become eventually as a complete person.

It would appear that from a counselling or listening friend's point of view, the task is to minister to those aspects of human nature that are there all the time, such as intellect or emotions, in such a way that they help the person eventually to become the complete person he or she is destined to become. With this in mind, we will now examine the standpoints of **being**, ie that which is given and is there from the beginning; and of **becoming**, ie that which a human being grows into, to become fully a person.

Nature and Nurture

One important factor in the development of personality is the Nature versus Nurture issue. It raises the question as to whether individual people's characters are like they are because they were born like it and inherited their vices and virtues (nature theory); or because their characters are formed by the influences of the social and physical environment in which they grew up (nurture theory). If the first is true, then all the effort that might be made in education, counselling and other supportive work, will achieve nothing in the long run; people will be what they are despite all that is done to help them, 'the leopard cannot change his spots'. If the second is true, then people are the victims of their environment, their characters are formed by it and we are all like a blank sheet of paper upon which the experiences of life write their own story.

It is easy to find advocates towards the extremes of both these views, but their inadequacy can be seen if they are simplified as in the analogy of the potter. Both these theories tell us that different potters with different types of clay will make non-identical pots; but they also tell us that the same potter with the same type of clay will make identical pots!

The table below shows how the nurture and nature theories differ:

POTTER	+	*CLAY*	➜	*POTS*		
				Nature	*:*	*Nurture*
Same	+	*Same*	➜	*Identical*		*Identical*
Different	+	*Different*	➜	*Non-identical*		*Non-identical*
Same	+	*Different*	➜	*Non-identical*		*Identical*
Different	+	*Same*	➜	*Identical*		*Non-identical*

The nature theory indicates that it is the nature of the clay that determines the outcome of the pot (whoever the potter). The nurture theory shows that it is the potter who determines the outcome of the pot (whatever the clay).

For centuries, the 'nature school' have tended to say, 'Some things are as they are, nothing we can do will make any difference. Slum parents will breed slum children, blue blood will breed blue blood'. The 'nurture school' has been a more recent development. Coming out of the enlightenment, the age of reason, it has always emphasised radical reform and changing the environment so that people can be released from destructive and bad environments to fulfil themselves. One big influence on this attitude has been the disciplines of psychology, especially psychoanalysis, and sociology. As with the Nature school, the Nurture school can point to evidence to support their view. It makes teaching, counselling and allied therapeutic efforts worthwhile because it gives them a rational possibility of success.

The fact that evidence can be found to support arguments for both of these views would indicate that neither on their own contains the whole truth; both contain elements of it. This is illustrated by the example of identical twins in a family from a poor inner city background. One becomes very successful, the other, very inadequate. This phenomenon is best understood by taking account of both the nature and the nurture theories. The difference between the two children lies in the complex interaction of inherited nature, their family nurture, and their response to both. The one who becomes successful developed a 'fight' personality, able to wrestle with the environment, using it as a grit in the oyster shell to make a pearl; whereas his sibling developed a 'flight' personality whose instinct was to escape and not make efforts in the unpromising environment. The latter type of personality is usually sensitive and collapses under a negative environment.

In conclusion, it would appear that our characters are built by a very complex interaction between nature and nurture. People are not blank sheets of paper upon which the experiences of life write a story. From conception they are complex and delicate living organisms which respond to the stimuli that come from their environment in a very wide variety of ways. Experienced helpers become increasingly aware of this, and the more case histories that are studied, the more the evidence for this complexity grows.

On the one hand, there are quite evidently certain patterns of behaviour that come from nature such as an exceptional talent for music, business, languages, art and so on. These seem innate in people and can be developed, or they are not there and nothing can be done to put them there. The same applies to environmentally learned patterns of behaviour that come from nurture; examples of these are crippling guilt feelings, feelings of inadequacy, aggressive, negative and compliant attitudes and so on.

With help, it is possible to change both nature and nurture characteristics or to modify them. To appreciate the complexity of the human personality, it is necessary to understand the 'being' and 'becoming' of the human person.

Being

The aspects of human nature which can be lumped together under the heading of 'Being' correspond roughly to Nature, in the Nature/Nurture issue. As already said, human beings are not just blank sheets of paper upon which the experiences of life write a story, thereby forming character. They are made up of very active and responsive raw material that can process the experiences of life, store some, reject others, and as a result of this interaction with experience, build up action and behaviour patterns of a complex nature that mould personality and feed the process of becoming.

It is evident that at conception the human being has the capacity for active response to the environment. Work done by Dr Frank Lake and the Clinical Theology Association, as well as the experience of many counsellors show this. A very common example is the person who is full of anxiety but is not sure what causes it. This is often expressed to counsellors in the following way: 'You see, I always have to find something to worry about, if it is not one thing, it is another'. Case history studies of such people nearly always show that mother worried and sometimes grandmother worried, and that the circumstances during which they were conceived and in the womb were threatening to mother, for example, babies born in the war during air raids, where mother was exposed to danger during pregnancy, illegitimate children, refugee children and those from families where there was tension and unhappiness for a variety of reasons. As adults these people carry a high degree of anxiety around with them.

Such people experience a great reduction in the level of their anxiety when they can experience stable, loving relationships with understanding people, and learn how to manage it. Anxiety itself is in us all and can never be removed. It is an example of something that is of the 'given' or 'being' in us that is not created, but activated by our environmental circumstances.

Anxiety is an example of an *emotion*, and emotions are feelings. Basically we do not think about them, we experience them, though we can learn to talk about them. However some of the more traditional approaches in education give little opportunity for the intellect to reflect on emotions. They can be described as the part of the human personality, or psyche, which experiences life. This experiencing does not just come through the five senses but through 'picking up the vibes' in situations, as the current phrase expresses it. If we are in a happy atmosphere, it is transmitted through the air to us. The same is true of anger, tension, sadness and so on. The emotions therefore both transmit and receive all kinds of feelings, either through the senses or direct. People vary in the way they are aware of this and also in the way they operate. It is possible to block off the emotions by incorrect use of the intellect when an individual cannot handle his or her own emotions. Some people seem more able to transmit and receive emotional stimuli through the senses than direct and vice versa, which results in a variety of behaviour patterns due to emotion. Understanding and handling emotions is one of the most important things a counsellor needs to do, and the following diagram shows how the emotions we have relate to each other.

Four Basic 'Given' Emotions

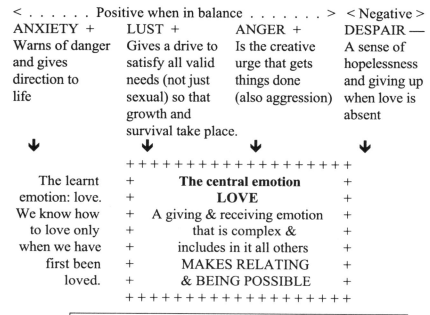

< . . . . . . Positive when in balance . . . . > < Negative >

ANXIETY +	LUST +	ANGER +	DESPAIR —
Warns of danger and gives direction to life	Gives a drive to satisfy all valid needs (not just sexual) so that growth and survival take place.	Is the creative urge that gets things done (also aggression)	A sense of hopelessness and giving up when love is absent
↓	↓	↓	↓

```
                    + + + + + + + + + + + + + + + + + + + +
  The learnt        +      The central emotion          +
emotion: love.      +             LOVE                  +
We know how         +    A giving & receiving emotion   +
  to love only      +         that is complex &         +
when we have        +      includes in it all others    +
  first been        +         MAKES RELATING            +
    loved.          +        & BEING POSSIBLE           +
                    + + + + + + + + + + + + + + + + + + + +
```

> Feelings of GUILT & SHAME develop as a result of the
> interaction between NURTURE and the
> 'GIVEN' BASIC EMOTIONS

> HATE
> The opposite of love
> always a counter response

Secondary Emotions that come out of Basic ones when they are either
not properly satisfied or not properly handled.

↓	↓	↓	↓
Self-righteousness	Greed	Violence	Mistrust
Critical attitude	Licentiousness	Rage	Self-pity
Panic attacks	Jealousy	Malice	Sadness
Uncertainty	Envy		Hopelessness
Hardness			

As well as emotions, human beings have other attributes; intellect, imagination, will, conscience and talents.

(i) Intellect

The intellect is the faculty of knowing by reason. It also allows us to interpret the messages that our emotions give us from what they are experiencing. Human beings experience first and think about it secondly. This is where problems can arise because most of the time, the intellect does not operate independently of the emotions. Where emotions are hard to accept or understand, the intellect, though in fact driven by them, tells itself it is not. René Descartes, founder of Cartesian philosophy, which set the tone for the modern scientific approach based on reason, did so by detaching intellect from emotion and thereby splitting the human personality. This has created an educational approach that can leave people psychologically unbalanced. In a healthy person, the intellect needs to be integrated with the emotions, and not given a value out of all proportion to the other human attributes.

(ii) Imagination

Imagination is the ability to perceive and understand our experiences by use of pictures and images rather than logical language. Dreams and daydreaming are the products of the imagination, some of which we can describe in words. Through dreams we can understand the subconscious, work out personal problems and make creative decisions by projecting ideas onto situations in the future. It is an essential component of the self-reflective ability referred to in Robert Burn's poem at the start of this chapter. This faculty is very active in children, especially at the play age, and helps them with their development as persons. It tends to become crushed by the excessive intellectualisation of our age, as we become adults. However, in very artistic people, imagination is sustained, and it is also greatly used in different kinds of therapy.

These three aspects of personality, (intellect, emotion and imagination) are inter-related, and, as a person develops, the will and the conscience appear to grow out of them. Thus, the will and the conscience are given only potentially and are developed through nurture.

(iii) Will

Will can be described as the ability to marshal one's forces and direct them in a positive way. The developing child learns to do this quite early in life and it is expressed by defying or testing out mother or father. Weak will is a result of lack of integration of intellect, emotion and imagination. Bad nurture undermines will; brain washing is aimed at doing this. The person with a strong healthy will can make decisions and carry them out, a weak willed person cannot.

(iv) Conscience

Conscience is similar to will and is our moral sense of right and wrong. It is developed by taking into our being parental messages received through both the intellect and the emotions. Some say that it is a purely nurture attribute of human personality, but, like the will, it is given in the sense of being potentially there and developed through the active response of emotions, intellect and imagination, and depends on their balance and integration for its growth.

(v) Talents

Finally, there is one more aspect that is given which seems to exist independently of those already mentioned. It is *talents*. Different people have different ones, and geniuses have exceptional ones, usually in particular directions. These can be developed, but they do need to be there in the first place.

Body and soul

All these personality attributes described are *spiritual* because they have no physical manifestations of themselves. Together they form a living person, or soul. A person resides in a physical body and is closely related to it in a similar way that clothes a person wears relate to the body in them. If the clothes do not fit, the body is pinched and hurts. The shape of the body also shows through the clothes. A person whose physical body is ill will feel it in the spirit through the emotions, and the way the person feels inside the body will show on the face. Such is the relationship between body and spirit, but the spirit is much more complex and less suited to scientific explanation than the body, which is understood by it very well.

I have chosen the approach that sees a human being as a living soul made up of a number of related and interacting parts because I think it gives a more realistic and less divisive model than the Greek one of body, mind and spirit. The idea of man as a living soul is Hebrew in origin and fundamentally religious, showing being to be about diversity within unity. This takes in all aspects and widens horizons. Materialistic views diminish human beings and leave out many important aspects of what makes us human, that complex and mysterious being, the depth of which at times seems to be unfathomable.

As a counsellor, it is with 'ordinary' people like this that I am in contact daily. Pain is always present in the human situation. It is very close to love and is present because we are emotionally complex. Little wonder that the cross is central to the Christian Faith and its understanding of ultimate reality.

Becoming

Having looked at being we now turn to becoming. The new born baby and indeed the foetus are living persons but they are only potentially the adults they might eventually become. The process of becoming takes place through interaction with the environment and a series of relationships with significant others, such as parents, siblings, school teachers and other authority figures, peer groups, aunts, uncles, and, for most of us, very important relationships with certain individual adults who happen to be there when we need them. This process has a common pattern consisting of stages that have to be worked through. These can sometimes be crises that have to be carefully negotiated or overcome.

A number of people have studied this pattern of development, including Erikson, Piaget and Freud. Their work has been brought together by Gordon Lowe in his book, *The Growth of Personality from Infancy to Old Age* (Penguin 1972). The map he charts based on their work will be our basis. *Human Development* (Allen and Unwin 1986) by Eric Rayner is considered by many to be a more satisfactory description of human development mainly because it is easier reading, but Gordon Lowe presents us with a better map which we will now follow.

Gordon Lowe gives us eight stages of human development, one more than Shakespeare's seven. The chronological ages are approximate, and must only be used for general guidance. Importantly, the stages of development indicate which stages must be worked through emotionally before the next stage can take place, and those relationships with others that enable them to do so. Where the environment of a child does not provide the right people for this to happen, then development is retarded, and they are likely to grow into insecure, unhappy adults.

The first three stages of development will be examined under the general heading of early childhood, the next two under the heading of late childhood and adolescence, and the final three under the heading of adulthood. At each stage, the relationships necessary for the emotional agenda to be worked through successfully will be described.

Early Childhood

(i)   The first stage in early childhood is infancy. It lasts roughly from birth until about two years of age. The most important person at this stage is the mother and this needs to be one person on whom the child can rely. For the first nine months or so after birth the baby does not know clearly where its being ends and its mother's begins. Prior to birth the baby is physically attached to the mother through the umbilical cord and its physical life is totally dependent on her. After birth its physical life is no longer fed by the attachment of the umbilical cord, but an emotional and spiritual attachment that is just as important and strong is formed with the mother person. This is called 'bonding' and is vital for emotional and spiritual development, hence Dr Frank Lake's description of this stage as the 'womb of the spirit'. If bonding is insecure and the mother person unreliable, the baby suffers. Its suffering is in the nature of spiritual and emotional pain. If this is allowed to continue beyond what is unendurable, neurosis develops, causing the child to become despairing and not able to trust. It will become a person full of doubts and anxieties about the world in which it lives. Gordon Lowe points out that the most important emotional issue to be dealt with at this stage is trust. The infant, if its experience is of consistent, loving and sensitive mothering learns that other people can be trusted and that the world is a safe place to be in. When this is not so, the infant develops a sense of mistrust which, if severe, can cast a dark shadow on the whole of its life. It is at this stage that the seeds of gloomy, pessimistic, doubting Thomas-type characteristics are sown, when a reasonable supply of good mothering is not given. Frank Lake expresses it thus:

> Acceptance of the potentially isolated, and, as such, anxious individual, by at least one other person, primarily by the mother, subsequently by the father, the rest of the family and society, is the primary ontological requirement. This access to human relationships ensures, on a personal level, his very 'being'. Without this he 'dies' as a person or as a member of society. Personal life is possible only when the seeking 'I' finds a 'Thou'. This alone makes possible the emergence of selfhood, of a steady functioning.
> (*Clinical Theology* p30, abridged by Martin Yeomans, Dartman Longman and Todd, 1986)

(ii)   The second stage of childhood is roughly from age two to four years. It is at this stage that the child should achieve a degree of independence from the mother and its relationship with the father becomes important. The emotional and spiritual issue to be achieved at this stage is autonomy – the stage of being in which an individual is aware of himself or herself as a separate being from others with an identity of their own, but is still in relationship with them. This identity includes awareness of themselves as a boy or a girl, and, a sense of knowing who they are and how to behave. Father is very important at this stage; he comes between the mother and child, modifying the close relationship of the first stage thereby helping autonomy to develop, and he also relates to the child as a being separate from the mother who is also different from her. By relating to father, the child is enabled to become involved with maleness. This involvement teaches the toddler how to relate to men and also is the beginning of it discovering its own sexuality.

When things go wrong at this stage, commonly through either bad fathering or an absent father, the child will be full of doubt about its own identity, especially its sexual identity, and will also have a high level of shame, being unable to 'hold its head high' through difficult times in later life. As a counsellor I meet many middle-aged people like this who were nurtured during the second world war when father was away. When he came back, they were already into the next stage, years five to seven, and unable to receive him into the kind of relationship they needed.

(iii)   The final stage of development in early childhood takes place roughly between the ages of five to seven years. By this time, the work within the basic nuclear family should have been done. It is called the social play age, as the children begin to play with each other (in contrast to earlier more private play) as a means of working out their emotional agenda and learning to relate to each other. At this stage the only child has problems because there are no other children in the nuclear family with which it can play and fight. Such children often have problems in relating to peer groups and can become withdrawn, anxious adults.

Infant schools now become relevant, which at an earlier age might have been a retarding influence by forcing the child to enter into relationships it is unable to cope with. Parents who leave their children in the care of others too early in life or too frequently can seriously damage them, because until a child has had time to work through all the relationships possible within the nuclear family it cannot cope with the ones outside. Early childhood ends when the child has done the necessary working out within the nuclear family and is eager to explore the world outside. Parents who have given the right attention to their children in the early stages will be able to read the signs of boredom which set in with reference to the home, and an eager initiative to get involved with children outside the home. Those who have not had the right environment within the nuclear family will lack this initiative. The shame and doubt about lack of the autonomy which should have been achieved at an early age will grow into feelings of guilt that are easily aroused. Infant teachers and play-group leaders will recognise this child as the timid, silent, withdrawn child who never does anything naughty. Superficial observation would see no problem because they are 'seen and not heard', no trouble at all; but wiser people would see them for what they are, and the naughty child as being more 'normal' at this stage.

In conclusion then, we can recognise the child who has been successfully nurtured through this period of early childhood because they are essentially enthusiastic, energetic, full of questions, keen to discover, responsive to a good story and able to bounce back when knocked off course. They will have been given many cuddles on mother's bosom, sat on daddy's knee, been tucked up in bed with a kiss, a prayer and a story; played, romped and squabbled with brothers, sisters, other children, mother and father; in fact experienced all the relationships, joys, tensions and sorrow that are possible within the security of a basic nuclear family.

The following series of diagrams illustrates the important stages of development in early childhood.

Stage 1
From conception to about 1 year

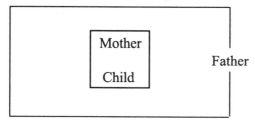

The child is unaware of any other person than mother in any real sense. Father protects mother and child from the stress of the outside world. A calm nursing mother gives the child a basic sense of wellbeing and trust.

Stage 2
Sometime between about one and two years old.

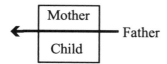

Father comes between mother and child as the first stage in helping the child to gain autonomy – i.e. become a separate individual.

The next three stages take place sometime between the age of two and seven. They are important for *sexual identity.*

Stage 3

The child becomes aware of mother and father being different and that they have a relationship.

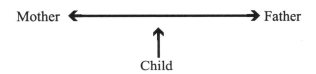

Stage 4

Child fixes for a time on mother to explore feminity.

Stage 5

Child fixes for a time on father to explore masculinity.

Male and female modelling are most important for a child. When they are absent or bad a number of problems can arise which affect the later life of a person, because they are unable to sustain committed healthy relationships with other adults, including that in marriage, and they may in turn provide less than optimum nurture for their children. The nurture in early childhood is the key to becoming a fully human person, and therefore the most important stage of our lives. The child we were is always alive in us for better or worse. The environment for this nurture is the basic nuclear family, hence the importance of the family for the individual's wellbeing on one hand, and its destructive power on the other, when things go wrong.

Late Childhood and Adolescence

In these two stages, the community outside the nuclear family plays an important role in development for the first time in a direct way. They can be called the semi-protected age because they are important stages between the protected development of early years within the womb of the nuclear family and the final launching into the world of the young adult. Adolescence can be very painful because it is a kind of birth into the adult world that comes at the end of this stage.

(i)   The **late childhood** stage is also called the school age or latency (dormant) period, lasting from about age six to twelve. School is the most important environment as far as development is concerned by stimulating growth, but the nuclear family remains important as a supportive base for encouragement and refreshment. 'Latency' refers to the fact that outwardly little seems to be taking place aside from physical maturation. Inwardly, however, something of great importance for the future is happening and it needs a settled home and school environment for it to be worked through.

Gordon Lowe lists the emotional issues to be dealt with at this age as being 'Industry versus Inferiority'. This means that the developing child needs to learn to apply itself to tasks and work at them until they are completed. If it does not achieve this it develops negative feelings of failure or inferiority. This can cast a shadow over adult life and many counsellors experience the pain of adults in middle age who feel failures because they have 'never made a go' of anything. Case histories of such people usually show a disturbed environment during the six to twelve age that seems to set up a behaviour pattern of inability to complete any task and a desire to remain a protected child. These low or non-achievers are not incapable people intellectually or as far as any other natural skills are concerned. Usually they had a very disturbed or unsettled childhood, perhaps changing schools several times. Wartime evacuees and children whose parents moved around a lot, eg forces' families, often produce adults with such difficulties. Thus we can see the importance of a stable home and local community environment to provide a safe launching pad for entering the birth pangs of adolescence resulting in fully autonomous young adulthood.

(ii)   The **adolescent** period of birth into the adult world takes place between the ages of thirteen and nineteen. It is the second most traumatic period of development after birth and a period in which review and recapitulation can take place. The individual gains an identity which gives a healthy independence from parents, clear sexuality (male or female) and a desire to understand and fulfil those roles in adult life. Where the environment of home and community does not enable recapitulation, this identity cannot develop for the individual and it results in an identity diffusion, shown in the person who is 'all over the place', being one thing one minute and another the next, totally incapable of firm healthy relationships with anyone.

As recapitulation is an important issue here, it would be appropriate to say something about it. In essence, recapitulation, or what we might call 'life review', is going back to emotional issues not properly worked out in earlier stages, airing them and working them out of the system so that one is free to move on. It is like a person moving house who has to decide what to leave behind and what to take to the next house. People for whom things went astray in the previous four stages now have a chance to put them right and leave them behind, so that adult relationships and attitudes can be taken up without overtones from earlier hurts and misconceptions getting in the way.

An example of how this could take place would be someone who had problems in infancy such as a difficult birth, inconsistent mothering or no real bonding with mother, will be aggressive to women and call their mother 'an old cow' or something similar. Older women who are motherly figures will be mistrusted. If these feelings can be expressed and worked out with loving mature adults then healing of emotions takes place.

Problems at the second stage are usually to do with fathering. Therefore adolescents need to argue a lot with their father. If fathers can recognise this, and are prepared to give plenty of time to arguing things out, then again, healing can take place. The arguments can be about anything, but it is the underlying emotional agenda that is as important as the intellectual content of the argument.

In the third stage, family rows triggered off by the adolescent are a way of working things out. The whole family needs to be involved here, and to act as enabling referees. Sometimes an outside but trusted friend can help. The rows are usually about things such as who has a bath at what time, coming in late, and 'If dad can do it – why can't I?' They often appear trivial but in fact have deeply rooted emotional content. These 'blow ups' are normal even though they can be distressing to both parent and adolescent.

Finally, the young adolescent may have to work things out concerning community, school, church, scouts, guides etc, that took place during play and school age. Much of this is expressed as anti-authoritarianism. This has roots usually in the relationship with the father, but not always. Knocking the system is the way it is worked out, and it can be done usefully in the context of debates and discussions in schools and youth clubs. What adolescents say during this period has validity in connection with personal development, but may not be very high in objective truth. The relationships they have with peer groups and adults who are models are most important, and therefore clubs relating to their natural interests are most valuable. This period of recapitulation is most traumatic because it is an unstable period in many ways. The physical body is changing, sexual awareness is very strong, emotions are powerful and unpredictable, the future is uncertain and everything new and exciting is calling for experiment. Because everything within the adolescent is in the melting pot, recapitulation is a possibility, but it can also be a threat. Without security provided by the mature adult world, it cannot be undertaken. The greatest need for adolescents is therefore mature adults against whom he or she can 'sound off' in a variety of ways. In general adolescents have an amazing capacity to select whom they need, but it is important that suitable adults are there for them to select. These adults must have an awareness of what is going on, and the grace that comes from real maturity to take the stress and stay with it. Adolescence can only be worked through successfully when the adult world in which the young person lives is mature and stable enough to provide the appropriate patient and supportive environment.

Adulthood
Finally we look at adulthood, the longest period of life. Here, although there is less emphasis on 'becoming', there are still two aspects in which adults never quite 'become', and as a result have a vague underlying feeling of 'if only' or 'ought'. There is also in many people a longing for perfection or completion which is elusive and never fully attainable in this world.

The feelings of 'if only' or 'ought' are often to do with unresolved issues of childhood. They may be worked through in middle age, and a middle age 'crisis' is a feature of many people's lives. It must be remembered that the child we were lives inside us all our lives and sometimes becomes emotionally dominant. This is the cause of many adult emotional problems, including those between adults and their young. Our parents are also with us all our lives because we internalise the messages they gave us during childhood. This may cause conflict if they are transmitted to others without any reference to the here and now situation, and those who transmit them, usually to their young, may be unaware of what they are doing. More will be said about this later.

The longing for completion or perfection is predominantly a religious issue. A sound spirituality is important for healthy adulthood, especially the last two stages – mature adulthood and old age. We need to continue our process of becoming until the day we die or else we become sour and negative.

(i) Adulthood has three stages. **Young adulthood**, roughly from the age of twenty to thirty or thirty-five, is taken up primarily with establishing oneself in the adult world. Competitiveness, and the desire for partnership and intimacy are features of this stage. It is the age of maturing and dating, getting married, setting up home and starting a family. At this stage, people should form some lasting intimate relationships and learn the skills of adult to adult relationships. Inability to do this leads to isolation and increasing loneliness, whether at home, at work, or in the neighbourhood, as the individual grows older. This inability always has its roots in unresolved emotional problems going back into childhood.

One important feature of this age is that so much energy goes into establishing oneself in the adult world that little is left for anything else. Getting married, caring for young children, passing professional examinations means that this can never be the age when it is wise to expect people to be available to help others in any deep way. They are not emotionally free, and without realising it, can only 'help' or be charitable when there is a pay off for themselves. This is not selfishness; it is tied up with personal growth and should be recognised as such. Otherwise, many conflicts may come in because the keen young person on the Parent Teacher's association, or some other body, will always use it as part of their own development. This is natural, and though perhaps apparent to others, it is usually not so to them until they get older and enter mature adulthood. The mark of the young adult is that they have something to prove, while the mature adult is comfortable to be without striving.

(ii)   **Mature adulthood** can begin at the age of thirty if all has gone well beforehand, but for many it may be long delayed. It is the longest period of life and gives way to old age at about sixty-five years. The behaviour patterns of young adulthood can persist well into this period, and so can those of adolescence. The marks of mature adulthood are; the ability to love and be loved, the desire to hand on skills and insights to younger people, and a general feeling of having found one's place in life. It is a time of coming to terms with one's limitations and accepting oneself as one really is rather than being competitive and ambitious to make one's mark as one is in young adulthood. At this stage the quality of spiritual life becomes important if degeneration into negative self-absorption and bitterness at the prospect of growing old and failing are not to take over.

The most positive aspect of mature adulthood is that it is the most creative and giving period of life. Erikson calls it the 'age of generativity'. It is the time when people have the resources to give of themselves both emotionally and spiritually without strings attached as in earlier stages. A person cannot become an effective counsellor or helper to reach people in deep distress until a good degree of adult maturity has been reached.

(iii)   **Old age** comes when the individual's physical strength begins to fail. It is a time of letting go in preparation for death, and, like adolescence, is a period of recapitulation. Here, it involves going over one's life to integrate all the stray bits so that they can make some sort of sense. That is why old people like to reminisce. This can be either a positive or a negative process. If positive, it enables the old person to be happy for both positive and negative processes that made him or her what they are now. The spiritual life is most important now because it helps old people to come to terms with death and see it more in terms of birth into a new life. The negative side of recapitulation is when the 'if only' attitude takes over. 'If only I was young again' or 'If I had life as easy as the young of today, I would be different'. This tends to create a very jealous and vindictive old person who is impossible to live with. Spiritual renewal, and the corresponding ability to forgive and let go the negative part, are the only hope for such people.

As has already been indicated, this negative attitude indicates something having gone wrong at an earlier stage of development and never having been put right. When this is the case in old age, it becomes a terrible burden for all around to bear. In my own experience of ten years as a chaplain to an institution for old people, I observed that many were there because they were too difficult to live with. They were like this because they had had a bad childhood and in return gave their children a bad childhood, mainly because they did not know any better.

In conclusion, this chapter is important. Firstly its contents will be used as a reference point when we talk about the practicalities of helping. Secondly, the main function of a family is to be seen as a place for the nurture of children into healthy adults. Thirdly, any would-be helper must become aware of their own development. Everyone has a hiccup somewhere, even the most 'together' person. This is inevitable because we were born into, and live in, a fallen and imperfect world in which things go wrong that we are powerless to avoid. It is not having a hiccup or flaw in our own development that disqualifies us from helping others; it is not being aware of it.

Chapter IV

The Nature of the Family and its Social Context

In this chapter the family is viewed from a social standpoint. As the nurture group in which the individual person grows and develops, its health is vital for their wellbeing. In this world, everything is connected to everything else, often in ways not overtly obvious. A baby, for example, is born tense and anxious because the mother was tense and anxious during the pregnancy. Mother was tense and anxious because the country was at war and the father had been called up to fight. The country was at war because some politicians, unknown to this family, made certain decisions, miles away from the community in which this family lived. Initially these decisions had no bearing on the family, but by a series of repercussions, the community, the family and finally the baby were drawn in. This simple example has many variations that are about the way in which political, economic, religious, racial and combinations of all these factors affect individuals and their families simply because of the way society is. This is a given, unalterable factor that must be taken into account by any helper of the family.

An understanding of the family as a social group within larger and less obvious social groupings, will help in the diagnosis of problems and give guidelines towards their care. Two illustrations of this point in the case of the anxious baby are, from one end of the social grouping spectrum, political avoidance of war and from the other, a mature and able woman from the community or extended family who can give immediate local assistance to the family. Both are valid examples of helping, one at the level of political action and the other at a warm personal level.

Political action is often the only way of providing the right environment in which families can be healthy, but of itself does not provide enough.

Caring and competent individuals can do a lot more when the social conditions created by the right political actions are good, but they can also do a lot in adverse social conditions.

Social groupings
When considering families as social groupings, it is essential to realise how important such groups are for our very being. Nobody can exist as a human being without belonging to some group or other. This is true of recluses and people who 'drop out' as will be seen more clearly later when the nature of groups is examined. Such people are using groups as a kind of launching pad into their chosen life-style which is a negative response against some group or other. Therefore without a group somewhere in the background of their lives they would not be able to drop out. Belonging to a group tends to happen in such a way that we do not always realise it. We are just born into a family which is set within a wider family, in a certain neighbourhood in a certain country and culture. This automatically puts us within several groups from our birth. The nature of groups is examined more fully in Part Three. Suffice it here to say that the nuclear family is the best example of a primary group.

Primary groups
Primary groups ideally contain ten to twelve individuals, although they may rise to as many as fourteen or fifteen. The positive nature and value of a primary group is that it is a group within which very intimate relationships can develop. It is a group in which individuals can work out their problems, learn to experience love and acceptance and thereby be encouraged and strengthened to face the stresses and strains of life. It is also a group which can be very creative, but for this reason it is potentially full of stresses and basically unstable.

It is quite natural for a primary group to come into being, function at a specific task for a certain period of time, and eventually die or disintegrate. Some primary groups can be so full of dynamic interactions between the members that they actually blow themselves to pieces and disintegrate rather more quickly.

The nuclear family

If we look at how nuclear families come into being, we can see all the aspects of a primary group, as it grows, develops, comes to a peak and then declines. A family begins when two people get married then children begin to arrive, usually one by one, until the full family has arrived. Then as the children grow and develop, there comes a time when one by one they leave home and establish their own individual lives, so that in the end we are left with the original couple who started the family. I am not saying at this point that the family ceases to exist in the wider sense, but in the narrower nuclear family sense. It ceases to exist because its function was as a support group for the family to grow and develop into complete persons. When this is completed they are then able to leave and go off, possibly to form their own nuclear families. So when the children have become adult, the primary group or nuclear family ceases to be.

During the process of growth in nuclear families, an enormous amount of re-adjustment needs to be continually taking place. The parent cannot treat the twelve year old the way the two year old was treated, nor can the twenty-five year old be treated as a tiny child any more; they must learn to relate equally as adults. So we can see that the dynamics of a small group as observed in the family are pretty demanding and continually changing. They are both supportive and exhausting; the two go together in a strange sort of tension.

The nuclear family needs the support of the extended family and the local community, acting as secondary groups, to give the individual members the stability they need so that the problems that come from the tensions within it can be turned outwards, helping personal growth to take place. It is important for any helper to understand the nature of groups in relationship to what goes on in nuclear families so that any problem is seen in its true light. We will now re-examine the developmental needs of the individual in relationship in the light of social groupings.

Life stages and social groupings

(I) Stage 1: Conception to two or three years

In the early stages of growth, from conception to two or three years old, the individual is only aware of its nuclear family; mother in the first place, then father, and thirdly brothers and sisters. However the well being of the nuclear family depends on many other groups to which it relates and this indirectly affects the individual child. Let us look at how this works out. (i) Primary groups. Both mother and father can be helped by belonging to such groups so that they can recover from the stress involved in raising the family. Father might go to the pub or club just to talk with a few friends. Mother might have her own groups to go to – keep fit, WI or a few friends – some evenings when father stays in. Sustaining close relationships with a few people outside the family is important for couples with children and for sustaining their relationships with each other. The following diagrams illustrate this.

1 – HEALTHY

Father

Mother

area
of
individual
interest

shared
area
of
responsi-
ibility

area
of
individual
interest

2 – SICK: Shared area of responsibility too large. Area of individual interest too small. Danger of one person crushing and demoralising the other. Bad modelling for child.

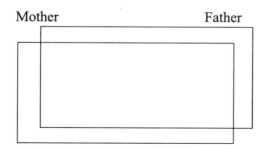

Mother   Father

3 – SICK: Danger of complete breakdown in relationship. Tension and insecurity for child.

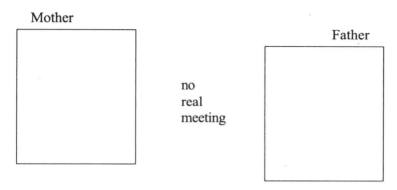

Mother

Father

no
real
meeting

Individual areas of interest are important to refresh and support both parents so that they come fresh to face shared problems and can nurture their young more efficiently. New experiences are fed into the family by each partner as they share conversations and good times they have had outside the family, with each other and the children. This kind of stimulus and deeper more personal issues can be helped by group contacts outside the family, and these are most important for its wellbeing. (ii) Secondary groups. These are important because they offer support to the nuclear family and individual parents at this stage, without close emotional involvement. They can also provide the milieu in which the type of necessary primary groups mentioned above can develop. Such secondary groups are:- the local community, extended family (grandparents, aunts, uncles, cousins, in-laws etc) and associations attached to places of work.

Because of the nature of secondary groups, people within them know each other but not at a very intimate level. This provides necessary relationships to balance the more intense ones within the primary group situation of the nuclear family. Aunts, uncles and grandparents should always stay as secondary group figures, because if they get too emotionally involved they are not able to render the relevant support. This involves careful consideration of the geography of dwellings to avoid the negative tensions caused when in-laws and other extended family members are too close to the primary family group.

All members of extended family, or local community, in attempting to help the nuclear family, must be aware that they are in fact members of a related secondary family group and not primary group members of the nuclear family to which they are offering support.

(II) Stage 2: Four to nineteen years

It is during this period that the nuclear family as a primary group becomes less important and secondary groups become more important. The interaction between primary and secondary group is most probably the main issue.

(i) Interaction between primary and secondary groups. It is at this second stage that a sound primary group is especially important, one which will continue to be sound in its support and understanding of the individual child, enabling it to fully benefit from the relationships in the secondary groups that it now begins to enter. From the members of the secondary groups to which it now belongs, it will begin to form the primary groups that will enable it eventually to survive the demise of its own nuclear family as a primary group, with a healthy degree of autonomy. At this period, the individual tends to be bounced backwards and forwards between its own nuclear family and various secondary groups, until it emerges able to form its own completely new primary group. This is illustrated in the following diagram.

	Primary group Nuclear Family involvement*	Secondary group involvement†
Play group	*****************************	†††††
Primary school	****************	†††††††††††††††††
Secondary school	************	††††††††††††††††††††††
Work/University		
College	*****	††††††††††††††††††††††††††††††††

This diagram shows how the importance of the nuclear family as a primary group diminishes as the child grows older, and the corresponding secondary group grows in importance. This process is rarely smooth and consistent. It happens more quickly for some than others, more easily, or more painfully, but it must happen and in most cases, the relationships between individuals and their nuclear families need to be re-adjusted several times as the individuals grow.

At playgroup age, approximately three years old, the child can only cope with a few hours a week outside its nuclear family primary group. However, when it goes to primary school, not only does it cope with longer times away from mother, but also makes significant relationships within a secondary group setting. These relationships are with other adults such as teachers who become new authority figures, and other children with whom it plays. The relationships formed with other children extend into the local community. Individual relationships and primary groups are formed outside the nuclear family that are important for the child's development, but the family is still the most important 'fall back' support group. This is shown by the way children at this age usually go over the top a little emotionally when they come home from school. As one little boy said, 'Well, daddy, I have to be naughty somewhere. It is such hard work being good at school'.

Until the child is most probably well into secondary school age, it is important that the home must continue to be a place to unwind and an effective primary support group, to allow the child to learn how to cope with secondary group relationships and be able to form its own primary support groups when adult. This is often evident in the case of non-coping adults who in the course of counselling were found to have been 'latch-key kids'. These people did not learn to cope in secondary group situations, because in times of defeat and exhaustion in the struggle to do so, had nowhere safe and accepting to fall back on, recover their energies, and then go back to continue the struggle involved in establishing themselves in the wider world.

Two other important issues for development are peer groups and significant others. These become progressively more important as the child grows older until adolescence when they are very high in priority. Peer groups are very important in adolescence because they are the person's main source of primary group support. They are formed from within the secondary groups to which the adolescent belongs. For this reason, youth clubs are very important.

(ii)   Peer groups. Many parents of adolescents are aware of the power of peer groups. Styles in dress, tastes in music and so on, are governed by what the peer group thinks and the opinions of the nuclear family, especially parents, are usually brushed aside. This is a valid part of growth; if it were not so, the young person would not acquire the strength to 'leave the nest' and become an adult. Again in counselling practice, one frequently comes across the anxious, inadequate adult whose personal growth has been crushed by an over-powerful nuclear family. Often the cause can be traced to adolescence when there was a failure to become involved in strong peer group activity.

(iii)   Significant others. For the adolescent, these are most important. They are models outside the nuclear family from which the growing person is able to take bearings that enable them to know their own identity. They are of two types. The first type are secondary group figures; aunts, uncles, grandparents, from within the extended family, or teachers, youth club leaders and other persons with status in the local community to whom the young person relates easily and with whom he or she can have heart to heart discussions about important matters concerning life.

The other type of significant other are tertiary group figures such as pop stars and sporting heroes. Youngsters often have their bedroom walls adorned with pictures of them. They take prime position and fall from grace (i) so rapidly that outwardly the adolescent appears very fickle. However, this appearance of fickleness covers a deep inner need that uses these hero figures as a means of forming their own identities, and they are (ii) also important in the formation of character and morals. They are tertiary figures because they are never known personally but are vehicles for the young person's fantasies and projections. 'I want to sing like X, or play football like Y' is often played out to the extent of imagining that they are the actual person. This can obviously become obsessive and sick escapism, but it also provides ambitious drive that can enable a young person to be motivated into developing his or her talents. The moral influence is very powerful in this area and points us to the importance of standards of morality at a national level, in all forms of life in the sporting and entertainment worlds, as a part of caring for the wellbeing of the family and young people.

(III) Stage 3: Adulthood
This stage can be divided into young adulthood, mature adulthood and old age.

(i)   Young adulthood (roughly the period of life between twenty and thirty years) is the final stage of becoming and the first stage of being, in which both are very closely interwoven. For this reason it is the stage when secondary groups are most important. The young adult has left the nuclear family primary group and is afloat in the world seeking to form his or her own new primary group for support during the long period of mature adulthood. This is usually by finding a partner and then marrying. Those who choose to remain single also need to find a primary group for support, and failure to do so can lead to a life of desperate loneliness and isolation; many young people living alone may find themselves in this position.

Of importance to the young adult are the qualities and content of the secondary groups of which he or she is a member. These need to provide a wide variety of people of the same age and stage of development so that relationships will be formed that will lead to suitable primary groups growing up for the next stage of life. In rural areas there is a standing joke about Young Farmers clubs being marriage agencies and the same can be said for many other institutions and places of work.

Another important factor at this age is the quality of mature adults available in the secondary group to whom the young adult can relate and from whom he or she can get the right kind of support and guidance. The mature adult needs to be emotionally strong enough to be used by the young adult as part of their process of maturing. Such people can help the young adult in many ways to discover his or own potential and realise it, and this can come about as much through conflicts as heart to heart discussions.

(ii)   Mature adulthood (roughly the period between thirty and sixty-five years) is the age where primary groups gain importance again and remain so for the rest of life. The majority of married adults will have young growing families, though still with a need for primary group relationships outside the nuclear family. Secondary groups form a stable background against which more intimate relationships of a primary group nature are worked out. Work, local community, church and a wide range of secondary groups will form an important part of the mature adult's life. The main quality of mature adulthood, described by Erikson as 'generativity' is exercised within these groups. The mature adult is a contributor, passing on skills already learnt in previous stages. It is within the context of groups that much of this takes place, and often from a leadership, or authoritative position within the group. This would indicate that youth leaders and people who run training schemes, workshops and so on, for the young should come from this mature group of adult people. It is a part of further education which should not be limited to universities and colleges, and is a mark of a responsible society to see that this need is met.

(iii)   Old age (roughly age sixty-five to death) is the autumn of life when strength declines and primary group support is very important. Tensions easily grow in families between the demands of the old and young, and an aged person rarely fits into the nuclear family primary group easily as a permanent member. The problem usually is that whereas the old like to see young children around and are cheered by them, they can only cope with small doses of their exuberant energy. The best primary group for support in old age is a peer group most of the time but with contacts from younger age groups in related secondary groups.

In families, young children can suffer and become emotionally disturbed by too many demands from elderly relatives, especially those who have not had a successful earlier life and lack a good primary peer group. As in adolescence, with the importance of youth clubs, also in old age, a peer group club is of great importance. The similarity of the group needs of these two groups is interesting. Both are at an age of birth into a wider and threatening world with many unknowns, the adolescent into the adult world, and old person into the unknown of the next. Both need the help of people who are not in their age group to run their clubs and do the things they cannot do; for the youth, a generation older and for the aged, a generation younger.

Meaningful personal relationships with individuals are very important for the elderly especially as they grow frail. As with young adults, their individual relationships grow out of secondary groups to which the person has belonged for some time, such as a small localised community or church. Elderly people who in adulthood did not belong to a community or for some reason have become separated from it, rarely find these important individual relationships to give them support and comfort in their declining years.

A final comment about support in this stage of life is that, as in infancy, governments (that is, tertiary group figures) can do much by creating favourable economic and social conditions in which care of the elderly by local communities and families can take place. The elderly clearly do not fit easily into the nuclear family of their children or grandchildren. Provision of homes for expert care will always be essential, and counselling is very important both for the elderly individual and the family that cannot cope with them when the decision has to be made about putting them into a home or looking after them themselves.

Aware helpers

More detailed and specific examples of problems will be given in later chapters but it is worthwhile saying now that there are several things the non-professional helper should note. The first is that helping with family problems is very diverse. There are many areas of activity, all of which are equally valid and none of which are a complete answer in themselves. For example, one to one counselling is not always the right approach. Sometimes the need is for a group, be it mothers and toddlers, youth group or old people's club. In other cases some political activity needs to be initiated either locally or nationally.

The would-be helper must have enough social awareness to guide people in these matters as well as a good knowledge of human development. This chapter and the previous one together form a map to which reference will be made in the following chapters which deal with more specific and detailed issues. At this stage it is appropriate only to say that the basic role of a helper is that of enabling the necessary change to take place in relationships within the nuclear family, so that individuals can grow into human beings that are fully human, and not be trapped in negative and destructive situations. Human life is largely about growth, and social interactions which take place within groups, as well as between individuals, are the means by which this takes place.

Chapter V

The Personal Qualities and Skills of the Helper

In this chapter both personal qualities and skills will be dealt with together because they are very closely related. Personal qualities and attributes consist of a mixture of factors, some to do with being, and some to do with becoming. A person who might be incapable of doing something at one stage of life, eg listening carefully, may be capable of it later. Vice versa, one who was able to do something at one stage eg solving quadratic equations, might later be unable to do so. As human beings we grow and develop in an amazing complexity of ways and potential helpers must be aware of their own particular stage of growth and development before they become involved with others. This puts limitations on everyone. For example, a young adult person may be very active in doing things such as organising social events, while a person in their sixties might feel they no longer have the energy to do this but because of their life experience could well support others by listening and giving comfort.

(i) Maturity and Generativity
A helper who is to be effective then, must have reached a good degree of maturity, able to accept their limitations and work within their confines. Wisdom needs time to develop, but time alone does not always bring it. The quality of the maturity is well expressed by Erik Erikson in his book *The Growth of Personality* as 'generativity'.

Erikson said that generativity was primarily concerned with the establishing and guiding of the next generation. A 'generative' person, must firstly have achieved a status of their own without the need for others to boost them, and be happy to operate within the limits of their own strengths and weaknesses. Fritz Perls, the originator of Gestalt

Therapy, is alleged to have said, 'I am me, and you are you. If we happen to meet, that's fine, if we don't, that's OK also'. This is another way of expressing this quality of generativity. It is an attitude that can let things be because it does not have the driving urge to prove itself always right at others' expense. Generative people tend to see their lives, not as a series of successes and failures, but as a series of experiences, both good and bad, from which it is possible to learn and enrich oneself. Secondly, the generative person is genuinely interested in others and in handing on the skills and insights they have learnt without strings attached. The spiritual dimension of this quality is well expressed in the prayer of St Ignatius Loyola:

Teach us Lord, to serve you as you deserve, to give, and not to count the cost: to fight and not to heed the wounds; to toil, and not to seek for rest; to labour, and not to ask for any reward, save that of knowing that we do your will.   Amen

These two qualities of character – self-establishment and concern for others – are always dominant in the genuinely generative person. They are important in a helper because they greatly reduce the need to receive status or a sense of well-being from the response of those being helped. This makes the helping more effective because the person being helped is being given the emotional space and freedom to become themselves. G R Lowe says:

Adults are the people on whom young children depend, against whom teenagers rebel, and from whom young adults may learn. To put it another way round, in very general terms adults are regarded by children as protectors who are omnipotent and omniscient; by teenagers as authority figures who are hide-bound and 'settled'; and by young adults as persons of influence to be emulated, and eventually supplanted.
          (*The Growth of Personality from Infancy to Old Age* p223)

This means that adults without a degree of generativity may, in relationships, find themselves threatened by either being made to feel very responsible for them if children, thought to be stupid and reactionary by adolescents, and finally, made to feel a non-entity by younger and more vigorous adults. Generativity then, is also required for the adults own wellbeing. They may otherwise either find contact with younger people too threatening, or subtly manipulate them to boost their own weak ego. An example of this is a case of a youth club volunteer who was chronologically of a generative age, but psychologically somewhere between adolescence and young adulthood. When he began to get involved in youth club work, at first his drive, energy and enthusiasm were applauded. However, a few months later the club had to be closed due to vandalism, severe damage and loss of control. The leader had lost respect and control because the young people saw him as one of themselves psychologically, and as a result treated him as such.

The main quality that arises out of generativity as a whole is the ability to love and be loved without strings attached. It is the generative person who does most of the giving of love in society, and the pre-generative person who mostly receives. That is the way things are and must be accepted. It is true that the generative person needs to receive love from others in some form of committed relationship, but this needs to be with other generative people, otherwise there is a danger they may seek love from a pre-generative person under the guise of helping them. This will tend to block the development of the younger person, causing many problems.

Generative loving of those in a pre-generative stage has its pain. Any loving parent of adolescent children will be aware of this, and effective helpers must accept this pain of loving as part of the cost of helping. Indeed, real loving always involves pain because loving involves giving of oneself. But only those who have received much can give much. A generative person is only generative by virtue of what they have received and can only remain generative by continuing to receive.

A question that will indicate how much healthy generativity a person really has is 'How much frustration, criticism, false accusation and general abuse can I take from others whom I try to help, without becoming vindictive and taking on a tit-for-tat attitude?' Those who have worked through a lot of their own growth problems, have healthy relationships with other generative people and are honestly aware of their own strengths and weaknesses will be able to take a lot of pain and retain a good degree of poise and confidence. Those who are not so healthy as helpers will soon get drawn into negative vindictive attitudes expressed by such sentences as, 'That's the last time I'll do anything if that's the way they show gratitude.'

As the prayer of Ignatius Loyola indicates, loving has its own pain. It is not that the generative person does not feel this pain; it is rather in feeling it they accept it as part of the cost of living and loving, reflect upon it, come to terms with it, and use it for their own personal growth.

(ii) Reflection

The ability to be reflective is another quality a helper must have. Without it a healthy generativity would seem hard to sustain. Reflective ability is an intellectual activity which enables a person to stand back from the emotional heat of a situation with another person with whom they have a helping relationship, and to think out carefully what is going on. This enables the relationship to be developed in a more positive way. Without it a potentially helpful relationship that started well can end in disaster with both helper and helped worse off than before.

In summary, it can be seen that 'generativity' sums up all the aptitudes expressed thus far, but another important attribute now needs to be considered separately. It is Faith.

(iii) Faith

The faith that is essential is a belief that in any helping relationship with another person, a process that will ultimately be for good is being worked out, over, above and beyond the efforts and capabilities of the helper. The helper then sees his or her involvement as not being the essential cause of the helped person getting better, but as in an assisting capacity or kind of catalyst that aids and encourages the process. This kind of faith is important for two reasons.

Firstly, for the benefit of the person being helped. The helper with this faith does not crush them by forcing ideals on them they cannot live up to, causing guilt because the person may not even be able to accept them. Nor will the helper with faith feel compelled to offer simple but inadequate solutions which confuse the situation by creating new problems, and result, as it must, in some kind of rejection that is felt strongly. Perhaps the most common example of this is when an extrovert person tries to help an introvert one, who, without being aware of it, seeks to force his or her extrovert approach to problem solving on them. The extrovert seeks to solve problems by taking action, making decisions and generally 'doing things', whereas the introvert, who needs long periods of time alone to work things out before taking action will become confused and annoyed, often feeling pressured and rushed. This often makes them both guilty and even angry, in such a way that their problem can appear insurmountable to them.

Secondly, helpers need this faith for their own benefit because it gives them the ability to accept their limitations in genuine humility, thereby freeing them from unreasonable pressure to succeed in an easy and superficial way. These pressures can destroy and sour people, rendering them unavailable to others in any really therapeutic relationship. The healing power of any relationship comes from the helping person's ability to stay with the other person's pain and suffering. It is beyond logical explanation of a rational kind, and attempts to give such explanations can hinder healing in the long term. A faith or metaphysical and spiritual dimension is essential therefore in any person seeking to be an effective helper.

In the 1960s Paul Halmos wrote in his book, *The Faith of the Counsellors*, that 'all counsellors seem to be imbued by sentiments of worthwhileness in giving personal service to others'. These sentiments come out of a faith that there is some purpose or process taking place in a counselling dialogue that is beyond the immediate of the situation and provides a motivation for doing it. He was speaking against the spirit of the age that said that all the resources we need to help others are within ourselves and can be understood rationally. Treatment can then be worked out systematically and applied successfully in a mechanistic way – a view still held by some. Paul Halmos points out that in counselling practice, nobody works like this, they only think they do. In many cases, people get better or solve their problems in a manner that is far more mysterious. What happens is that someone loves a person in need of help, commits themselves to them in some kind of counselling contract believing they are worth bothering with, endures the pain of doing this, perhaps prays for them and at times despairs of anything positive happening. Nevertheless, over a period of time, a number of things happen, most of which are beyond the control of the helper, some of which are beyond explanation, but together forming a process which leads to the solving of the helped person's problems. My experience is that often the 'solution' is nothing like the one expected in the first place.

The person who can accept and understand this will be an effective helper, because they will be open enough in their attitudes to allow the people they are trying to help to grow and develop in their own way towards their full potential. They will be aware that some process is taking place that is beyond themselves and the person being helped. This process is good and beneficial, aiding the healing and in some way the helper is just enabling it to develop in its own way.

The development of pastoral skills

In dealing with this subject, the work of C B Truax and R Carkhuff is most pertinent because it shows a direct link between personal qualities and attributes, and skills that can be taught. They demonstrate that the one grows out of the other, and that it is possible to teach skills that are ineffective or even dangerous when the person to whom they are taught is not of a suitable personality. Academic, or taught skills on their own do not equip one person to help another, but when they are taught to those with the right basic qualities and attributes, they can sharpen and develop appropriate helping skills that are innate within that person's character. Not everyone can or should become a helper-counsellor.

The method used by Truax and Carkhuff was to examine a very wide sample of people who had sought help with their problems in order to find out what it was that actually contributed to their improvement. This examination was exhaustive in its thoroughness and when it first appeared in the USA during the 1960s caused quite a stir because it showed that academic training and professional rigour made little or no difference to the outcome of the help offered. In some cases, highly qualified people actually made the people they sought to help worse; but also large numbers of people seemed to work their problems out and get better without resorting to any form of professional help. This work done in America is also consistent with that done in England by H J Eysenck of London University whose sceptical views about the effectiveness of most forms of psychiatry, including many counselling methods are well known. This issue will be discussed later when we look at the relationship between the professional and non-professional helper. It must however be noted that there is much evidence pointing to the fact that academic and professional qualifications, of themselves, do not make people professional helpers.

Truax and Carkhuff discovered that there are six factors that need to be present in any relationship between people in a helping situation if the outcome was to be a good one, namely, beneficial to the person being helped. They also noted that these same six factors were equally essential in both professional and non-professional helpers. The factors were not related to academic qualifications, method of training or belief system of the helper. The conclusion was that where all six were present the outcome was good, where they were not it was bad, regardless of the status of helper.

People were selected for a training scheme lasting one hundred hours, who possessed the character attributes contained in these six factors, called 'the six basic dimensions of effective counselling'. They were given some basic theoretical training and helped to perfect the six factors already present in their characters. It was found at the end of their training that these people were able to produce counselling skills that matched those of the most skilful and effective professionals, whatever academic qualifications they held.

Let us now turn to these six basic dimensions.

The Six Basic Dimensions of Effective Counselling
(i) Empathy   (ii) Respect   (iii) Concreteness
(iv) Genuineness   (v) Confrontation   (vi) Immediacy

(i) Empathy This is the quality of being able to get alongside people without being so drawn into their pain that one becomes bogged down with it. Sympathy is not very helpful because it means suffering with the other person. The sympathetic person usually gets so drawn into the other person's emotions that they lose the ability to think clearly, and are rendered incapable of helping beyond sympathising. A totally emotionally remote person, would, on the other hand, remain too distant to help, and thereby become equally ineffective for totally different reasons. Empathy is a difficult middle course and can be like walking a tightrope. The following analogy illustrates what true empathy is like. A person is walking along a road; on either side is a deep, muddy ditch. In the ditch is another person, thoroughly stuck, struggling and crying 'Help!' If the person walking down the road is sympathetic, he or she immediately thinks, 'Help, there is some poor person in the ditch. I must do something!' and jumps in the ditch with them. End result – two people in the ditch. On the other hand, if the person is non-sympathetic and possibly afraid of getting stuck in the ditch, they will pass by without getting involved, on the grounds that they are not the right person to help, or too busy, or it is the other person's fault they are stuck in the ditch. The empathetic person however, on hearing the cry for help thinks, 'What can I do in this situation?' Then they go to the edge of the ditch, carefully look for a good foothold on the bank, make the foothold secure and then hold out a hand to pull the other person out of the ditch.

Empathy can be developed to a very high degree if the potential is already there. The training required, which will be covered later, must be based in experience, done in groups and not too academic.

(ii) Respect This quality allows the helper to accept the other person as they are. It says to them, 'You are free to be exactly who you are without the risk of being blamed for what you feel'. This enables the person being helped to tell their own story honestly, without the need to cover up anything. For most people this is a big issue because we are all conditioned to some extent to deny the truth about ourselves in order to be accepted. Many problems people have, such as reactive depression and anxiety about coping with life, have their origins in this big 'cover up plot'. Helpers having this quality of respect are 'easy to talk to' because the person seeking help does not feel morally censured and inferior. In such situations the truth is poured out, providing the possibility of an accurate understanding of the situation. Accurate understanding is the first requirement for solving any problem. Respect is an extension of empathy and together they form an essential first stage in any counselling or helping arrangement. When they are not present in the helper, people will not open up, or even talk at any depth. However, if these are the only two qualities a helper has, any helping situation will soon become bogged down and end in frustration. This negative situation is prevented by the presence of the next quality.

(iii) Concreteness This quality enables the helper to get the other person to tidy up their story, so that the real issues, the side issues and the false feelings, are clear in both the mind of the helper and the one being helped. Concreteness requires the helper to take a more active role, questioning the person being helped. Concreteness must always be preceded by empathy and respect. If not, it will have nothing to work on and make 'concrete', or firm and plain in the minds of both helped and helper. This quality is more dependent upon training and practice than the first two. It is also related to the person's reflective ability, that is the ability to stand back from the heat of the emotion in a helping relationship, to think clearly, ask the right questions and form an accurate picture.

(iv) Genuineness This quality is present all the time in the background. It is simply being authentic as a person and not putting on an act. When people come to anyone for help, they tend to put that person in an awkward situation. The first reaction is to adopt a stance that makes us feel safe, either by being self denigrating and apologetic, or by becoming very competent, pretending to understand everything. This is a defence against our own fear of involvement with a troubled person. Genuineness is the quality that allows us to be ourselves as helpers and be genuinely human. It is something that training can develop in a truly generative person because at its basis is self confidence.

(v) Confrontation This can be described as a development of concreteness. It is the ability of the helper to draw the attention of the person being helped to contradictions, ambiguities and unnoticed strengths and resources within themselves. It comes into play late in a helping relationship, and only when the helper, by using a good deal of empathy, concreteness and respect has uncovered the whole story and has had time to ponder upon it. Training is necessary to develop this quality until it becomes a very skilled art. As with concreteness, a clear intellect and a good reflective ability are at its basis.

(vi) Immediacy   Like genuineness, immediacy must be present all the time during a helping relationship. It is a continual awareness on the part of the helper of what is going on in the relationship. It relates closely to empathy, but is more than empathy because it must include negative feelings the helper may have, such as 'I wish you would go away now, I want to listen to The Archers'. This awareness guards all the other qualities and prevents the helper being forced up blind alleys that raise negative emotions in the course of the helping relationship.

Training helpers:
I now wish to outline a simple, but I hope effective plan for training helpers on the basis of what has been previously been said. The method will be a combination of experiential work and theoretical instruction set in the context of a small group of between eight to ten people. The qualification for people joining the scheme must be that they are the kind of person to whom people talk. This is not the same as people who like talking, who are usually unsuitable. A good question to ask is 'Are you a person whom others seek out to talk to even when you are not particularly interested in having a conversation with anyone? If your answer is "Yes", then join a group to find out why and develop your understanding of people and human relationships'.

This kind of approach should draw out those with potential as effective helpers, and from this starting point the six dimensions of Truax and Carkhuff can be developed, first theoretically, and then through practical group work. Firstly, the six dimensions should be thoroughly understood and internalised, so that they become like an aspect of our personality.

The other theory to be learned is the contents of chapters two and three of this book, with as much relevant reading as an individual feels able to cope with. Understanding the grief process is also important, and will be dealt with later. Initially, about ten to twelve group sessions lasting two or three hours will reveal those who are struggling to cope with the demands of serious helping. Those wishing to go on further need to belong to an ongoing support group that meets monthly. Those who do not cope with the strains and stresses involved in helping should not be discarded. I have run groups in which such people eventually learn to become effective helpers or have accepted readily some sort of supportive role, often administrative, in which they are happy. Skilfully led groups are a very good way of ensuring that failure can be faced and worked through to the benefit of the person who feels a failure.

In practical training, the group should be made up of even numbers, eight, ten or twelve, excluding the leader or trainer. This enables listening and responding exercises to be done in pairs, leaving the leader free to observe and exercise control so that the people in the group feel safe to open up.

The trainer/leader must insist on total confidentiality within the training group. This will stop destructive gossip about people in the group happening outside. It is important to present cases of current clients because hypothetical simulation does not develop skills or understanding in the same way. Honesty is essential. Group members must say exactly how they feel about those they seek to help and learn to get out all the facts so that the group can examine them and feed back insights. Respect, immediacy and genuineness must be observed at all times within the group. Being in the group not only sharpens helping skills, but enhances the participants' personal growth.

Diagram illustrating training method

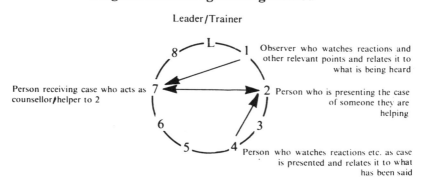

Leader / Trainer

8 — L — 1 Observer who watches reactions and other relevant points and relates it to what is being heard

Person receiving case who acts as counsellor/helper to 2 — 7

2 Person who is presenting the case of someone they are helping

5 — 4 Person who watches reactions etc. as case is presented and relates it to what has been said

If the case being presented involves other people such as mother, father, sister, brother, friend and so on, other members of the group can be asked to respond as though they were that person. This enables the helper to get a fuller view of the problem of the person they are trying to help and increases the skill and insight of those playing the roles of the others. The leader must be naturally skilled in handling group work as well as being an experienced helper.

Finally, listening and responding exercises are very beneficial, and simple to set up. One method is to ask people to talk to a partner about any incident in which they have been involved in the last few weeks. It could be anything such as buying a new coat, going to the theatre, losing keys in a supermarket, and so on. The person listening to the other person's story then practices putting into effect the Six Basic dimensions and the person telling the story becomes aware of how it helps them. Both should be aware of the feelings involved surrounding the 'facts'.

Another method is more difficult and aimed at bringing out deeper feelings, often of a negative type. It is the same as the first one, but the pairs sit back to back. The absence of eye contact means that understanding of the other one is diminished because body language such as the facial expression, movement of hands feet and so on, cannot be seen. On the other hand, feeling the vibes becomes enhanced and this is an important aspect of the helping relationship. When we lack, or artificially cut off any one of our senses, we help the others to grow, as any blind or deaf person knows. These exercises practised under competent supervision are necessary basic training for helping people to relate to others in a meaningful and therapeutic way.

The relationship between the professional and the non-professional
This is a very important consideration because the professional and the non-professional are very dependent upon each other, and yet also may come into conflict with each other. The helper to whom this work is directed is non-professional. This could cause professional helpers to feel that these amateurs have insufficient training and if encouraged too much will do a lot of harm. Also, very competent non-professionals can threaten over-worked hard-pressed professionals by undermining their status.

The work of Traux and Carkhuff shows that professionalism, with all that that entails, does not of itself bring about competence in helping. However, it does not deny the value and place of professionalism in helping people; rather it shows its limitations. If we are to create the right balance between professional and non-professional helpers both must accept the limitations that are placed upon them, then each can respect the other's role within the wider concern of helping people to overcome their problems.

What are the limitations? Firstly, the professional can become remote from the world in which their clients live by becoming over-involved in their own expertise and no longer able to relate as a human being to their client at their real point of need. A professional can also become isolated, unsupported and expected to achieve things outside their own expertise. (see, for example, Clark L, BAC Journal, August 1966)

Secondly, the non-professional does not have the expertise of the professional, and needs to be aware of this. They do, however, have that wider knowledge of life outside the counselling situation which is important and so often denied to the professional. They have an informality of approach, time to chat, and most importantly are always the first contact with the troubled person. If the non-professional is well trained in listening skills then they will be able to get an accurate picture of the problem, and know whether it needs to be referred to a professional or whether they can deal with it themselves.

The non-professional then, is a kind of first-aider who works in support of the professional. Their role is crucial because they are in touch with problem situations first hand in a way that the professional can never be, and even when a person is receiving professional help they still need the friendly day-to-day support of the non-professional. Being non-professional is not second class; it involves skills common to all helping relationships right across the board. It also involves having enough theoretical knowledge and insight to know when to ask for more professional expertise for a particular problem and to make the necessary arrangements.

Chapter VI

Some Likely Problems in Family Relationships

This chapter is intended to give the helper some idea of the kind of problems that will be met in trying to be helpful in the support of families. These problems will be put into two categories: those for whom the helper is adequate to cope as long as they can accept the pain and stress involved, and those for whom expert advice needs to be sought.

PROBLEMS IN WHICH THE HELPER IS ADEQUATE
These are problems mainly to do with the growth and development of individuals within the family as a basic nurture group. The two most important factors here are: the skills and qualities of the helper as a person, and their knowledge of human development and the place of social structures in this process, which will enable them to have an accurate understanding of the problem. The helper must always take care to understand the exact nature of the problem by the process of listening and questioning. The 'map' already given must be firmly in the mind as a point of reference, but the relevant information must be gathered carefully. The helper should be wary of sharing too much of his or her own experience.

Sharing and confidentiality
Nothing of the helper's experience should be shared at the early stages until the picture is clearly seen. When a decision about the remedial course of action is made, it can be helpful and appropriate in some situations to share experiences. For example, where the helper is a mother whose children have now grown up and doing well, and the problem situation is a rebellious and difficult teenager. The helper can say something to the other like, 'Mine were just like this (giving a

description of the problem) but now we have almost forgotten that it ever happened'. This encourages the mother of the present teenager not to despair by giving her the hope that the present suffering can lead to something fruitful in the future.

In this issue of adequacy, confidentiality is very important. This means that nothing at all must be said to anyone else. The totally sealed lip is essential and the person who enjoys a little gossip or joke about other people's misfortunes will soon lose respect and fail as a helper.

There are two areas where the confidentiality should not be the 'sealed lip' kind. The first one is in the context of training, support and reference to an expert for help. If therefore a person feels a burden of something told to him or her in confidence, sharing it with the group is not a breaking of confidence. It may be the only way the helper can cope with it. It is most unwise for the helper to say to the person being helped, 'I could not cope with what you told me so I shared it with the group'. This can ruin the therapeutic nature of the relationship because the person being helped may need, for the time being, an authoritative support person as part of the healing process.

In cases where the burden on the helper is too great and the support group points this out, the helper must go back to the person being helped and say, 'Your problem is too much for me, I would like to hand it over to someone more experienced. Are you happy with this?' People in trouble will nearly always agree in such cases, but there may be feelings of resentment around to deal with, and perhaps feelings of failure on the part of the helper, for which they will need support. For the helper, this is also a point from which their own growth and self awareness can be developed by working in a support group.

The second area is where what one person in a family is saying needs to be interpreted to another in order to help their relationship develop. This is a rather more dangerous area needing some positive manipulative skills. The basic aim is to hold other members of the family off the person being helped to give them the space they need, free from pressure, to work on their problem. The helper does not break confidence by giving away in precise detail what has been shared, but says something like this to the other family members. 'You know, George has been telling me a lot recently. Well, he has told me things which indicate that he should be left alone to work them out. Please do not pressurise him for the next few months, just let him be. I know you care about him but there are certain things he needs to sort out in his own mind before he can be himself again'.

This approach is often necessary in families where personal relationships are intense, and it can come near to breaking confidence, but not to do it can block out the healing process. It is also manipulative, and we must remember that not all manipulations are bad. They must be done well and in love to be really effective. The words of Jesus Christ are apt here, 'Be wise as serpents and innocent as doves' (St Matthew chapter 10 verse 16).

Grieving and loss

This is a recognisable process which happens in a person in response to the loss of something or someone that has been of deep emotional significance for them, to which, or whom, they have been deeply attached. This loss takes place fairly regularly during the course of our lives, nearly always within the context of our families. The most obvious and severe grief reactions are those concerned with the death of a loved one, husband, wife, child, mother, father, brother, sister, in most cases, but people can have very strong attachments to grandparents, cousins, aunts, uncles or even a non-blood relative who has become significant for them. Divorce and marriage breakdown can also be included as a source of grieving. In all such cases of grief the important factor is the loss of the person who has been significant to them in their growth as a person and their security in this world.

Another loss factor which is less often recognised is the loss of a secure situation due to growth, time or circumstance. Starting school, leaving home, losing a job, becoming ill are just some of the examples of how grief reactions can be set off in a person.

A third kind of loss can be related to moving home, changing jobs, being burgled, the death of a pet animal and any other loss of material possessions or material circumstances. It must be remembered that it is not only the loss of people, relationships and personal misfortune that is obvious, which causes grief reaction. Sometimes the loss of something may on the surface seem insignificant, a trivial and easily replaceable item in a burglary or accident, a key-ring, a cheap mug, or a picture of no artistic value, but the person concerned focuses all their grief on them. A helper should never say something like 'Don't worry, we can easily get another, they don't cost much', but instead encourage the emotional reaction, listening and seeking to understand what is going on behind this apparently superficial reaction.

Finally, grief reactions can be set in motion in a person by an awareness of something from the past that they have desired but never had, or an awareness of past hurts that have never been grieved because at the time they happened, grieving was either not possible, or not permissible. These reactions can be set in motion by watching TV plays and programmes, going to the cinema or theatre, seeing incidents which trigger off memories, or just by chance remarks made during normal social chit-chat. Again there are a wide variety of causes for such reactions from an unhappy childhood, misunderstanding by school teachers, and especially vulnerable in this area are the many men who have had bad experiences during military service.

This is a very broad but necessarily sketchy outline showing how widespread grief reactions are, so that the helper can be aware enough not to come in too quickly with answers and comments that will be valueless and in many ways harmful. The helper must, in helping such people become a kind of midwife, who enables an 'emotional' process to work its course in the afflicted person so that at the end of it new hope and life can grow.

Grief stages

I now want to outline the normal process of grief so that it can be firstly recognised and then enabled by the right course of helping. It can be said that for practical purposes there are three stages through which the grief process passes, although it can be more complicated than this.

The first stage of grieving is marked by numbness, listlessness, and a sense of meaningless disbelief. Nothing seems real for the afflicted person. They are in a state of shock and usually disorientated. At this stage a helper can only offer practical support and help, taking the person who is afflicted metaphorically by the hand and helping them to cope with the necessities of living. What matters most to the grieving person at this time is that there is someone who cares, is practical and reliable, but who does not hassle or pressurise them. The helper at this early stage should expect nothing of the grieving person or seek to try and give reasons for what is happening because there are no rational explanations that will make sense.

The second stage is one where the sufferer begins to react emotionally and comes in if during the first stage nothing has been done to cause repression, such as helpers being overbearing, saying too much, exhorting them to 'pull themselves together' or the doctor giving too many drugs to sedate and thus mask a perfectly natural process. These emotional reactions can be very strong, often with large amounts of anger, false accusations of others, tears, self pity and 'if only' remorse. They must be allowed to happen with no comment at all, no moralistic judgements or attempts to explain why. The helper should even encourage this expression, and when it has run its full course, the grieving person will begin to talk more rationally and even say things like 'I was silly to blame so and so. I can see it all now, but at the time I felt so angry'. When this happens it is a sign that stage two has been worked through.

Stage three is a more rational stage and it is at this point only that the helper can give their opinion about questions raised by the grieving person and help them re-orientate their life so that they can live realistically within their present situation. This stage will come automatically when the previous two are allowed to happen without anything inhibiting their process. Often because in severe cases, grieving people can inflict much pain and inconvenience on those around, stages one and two become repressed by use of drugs, moral exhortations and so on, that are in fact the defences of others against experiencing the pain of the grieving person. This danger is always a threat to real helping and must be honestly faced.

The time period for each stage varies, often according to the degree and type of loss that triggered off the process. Stage one can last up to a month, stage two several months, and stage three within a helpful environment is usually reached after six to nine months. The key to helping is to have enough patience to allow the process to happen, and enough personal security to cope with the pain and inconvenience involved so that the helper's own defences do not come into conflict with the emotions of the grieving person and hold the process back. In some cases of bereavement, unresolved problems from the past come up and get mixed in with the grief. These need to be recognised and dealt with separately. Being in a good support group will give the helper the guidance needed when this happens.

Projection, Transference, and Countertransference

These three concepts go together and it is important that the helper has a good understanding of them especially of how they happen in practice. It is in practical group training of the kind mentioned in the previous chapter that recognising them can be learned. First of all, the concepts need definition.

(i) Projection: The unconscious process by which an individual attributes to another the desires, impulses or ideas that he finds unacceptable in himself.

(ii) Transference: The term literally means to convey information or content from one person, place or situation on to another. The psychological usage expresses a special type of relationship with another person. The usual pattern is for a person in the present to be experienced as though he or she were a person from the past. This was first identified and developed by Freud. He was aware of the need for both in successful therapeutic work, but viewed it as a constant danger, feeling that it contained the potential for catastrophic consequences in therapeutic counselling.

(iii) Countertransference: This takes place when the transference is accepted by the therapist/helper as though they were the actual person from the past. For example, a person deprived of mothering in the past makes the therapist a mother figure, and the therapist accepts this role in a way that is negative and blocks progress, behaving as a mother in relationship to the person being helped, often to satisfy their own unfulfilled needs.

An understanding of these three ideas is important when a counsellor or helper comes up against the phenomenon of projection. It amounts to being blamed and feeling guilty for the faults, failings and predicaments into which those they seek to help get themselves. This is because an incompetent person gains a lot of kudos by having someone else to blame, or to see as being less competent than themselves. We all do this to a certain degree in order to survive. Moans about the government or anyone in authority contain a lot of projections. A helper needs to reflect carefully on the projections made both against them by others, and also by them against those whom they seek to help. A helper who understands projection is able to allow members of a family to moan to them about other members of the family in such a way that they 'get it off their chest', and are able to go back and cope with the family situation. One who does not so understand will take things too seriously, act upon them and make them worse.

An important function of the helper is to accept the individual's rubbish that is dumped on them by projection because it is often by allowing this that the family is able to continue functioning as a nurturing unit. Projections must never be taken as objective fact, they tell us more about what the person who makes them feels about the situation, and what they are afraid of. Often a person who is sent by the family to see a helper is not the problem, but the family's scapegoat on whom the family's unbearable pain has been projected. (See for example R D Laing, *The Politics of the Family*, Pelican, 1978).

Transferences also need to be worked with and understood. People being helped always transfer to the helper a wide variety of feelings which relate directly to the nature of the problem for which the person is seeking help. Simple examples are: a child of a single parent family whose lack is fathering will see a male helper as a father; a lonely elderly childless couple could see the helper as the son/daughter they never had. There is a infinite variety of subtle transferences and a wide variety of roles put upon the helper: authoritarian figure, Guru, or even a kind of god to lover playmate wife/husband, or fellow sufferer.

The above examples are positive transferences because they put the person in a good light in the eyes of the person being helped. Negative transferences occur when the helper is seen as being just like some person in the past who has caused hurt. When this is so the helper is rendered ineffective unless the negative transference is overcome. It is possible to do this if the helper picks it up and says something like 'Anne, I feel that you have a certain hostility towards me and I cannot work out why it is. Could it be possible that I remind you of someone from the past with whom you did not get on?' Often this will elicit a response like, 'Yes, my mother'. If this is so then the relationship with the offending person from the past can be discussed and the transference problem solved. If this is not so, then in many cases the helper must bow out and find someone else to deal with the person seeking help.

Having recognised a transference, then the helper must decide if a countertransference is likely to happen. If the transference is a bad one, where the helper is being felt to be a bad person like the one from the past who hurt them, then the helper cannot accept the role. If it is accepted then the helper is caught in a countertransference because they unconciously act out what the person being helped makes them. They must say firmly, 'I know that something about me reminds you of X who hurt you and always made your life difficult, but I am not X or anything like him/her, so let us get him/her out of the way so that I can relate to you as I really am'. From this point the helper will need time, patience and perseverance in developing a positive helping relationship.

If the transference is a positive one, then it can be accepted and used positively if the helper is wise. The way to do this is to spell out the situation and make a contract. This will prevent a negative counter-transference that makes the person being helped totally dependent upon the helper. The helper could say, 'Fred, I am aware that you never had an effective father and that you see me as your father because of this. I am not your real father and never can be, but I am willing to stand in as such for the time being to tide you over your problems and help you to stand on your own feet. Shall we agree to this and make some practical arrangements to carry it out?' This contract must be continually reviewed in the relationship.

People who are able to understand and cope with projection, transference and countertransference can help enormously in completing the inadequate nurture caused in families by a variety of unfortunate mishaps such as untimely deaths, lone parent families, sibling rivalry and allied conflicts, social disruption, poverty, inadequate parenting, mental illness and a whole host of others. The helper in effect does this by becoming a substitute mother, father, grandfather, aunt, uncle, brother, sister, or general confidant and trustworthy friend. But they must know what they are taking on and make an appropriate contract.

CONTINUING SUPPORT FOR THE HELPER

In conclusion, the key factor in preparing helpers to deal with the many problems that are in the capacity of the non-professional, and indeed often best dealt with by such a helper, is continuing support. This enables the helper to wrestle with new situations when and where they occur and in so doing develop their skills and insights together with their own personal growth. Groups of the kind mentioned in chapter IV are the best setting for this on-going support. Where this is not possible, individual supervision is useful, but does not provide that same range of insight. In the context of a support group, helpers can find the answers to such questions as, 'How long do I need to go on helping this specific person?' 'Am I using the person I am helping to satisfy my own emotional need?' 'Should I be more or less directive?' 'Would this person be better helped by joining some social group or support group than by my individual efforts?'

These questions are all individual situations which need to be dealt with separately. There can never be 'answers' easily summarised by a formula, or in the pages of any book.

PROBLEMS FOR WHICH EXPERT HELP IS REQUIRED

Problems requiring expert help and referral can be put into two categories: those for which an expert individual needs to be consulted, and those for which a specialist group or social support is required. The helper needs to recognise them and enlist the appropriate help. Sometimes the family or individual concerned may not wish to co-operate, or even deny the need. If this is the case the helper cannot force the issue but should always make their opinion clear to all concerned and state that the problem is beyond their own coping ability. This is important because it prevents anyone from having false expectations of the helper and then at a later stage feeling let down and blaming the helper. The helper's support group is important in such cases because they help the helper to recognise the area of need and the relevant source of help. Here follows a list of such problems with hints to help with their identification and the appropriate source of help.

(i) Addictive problems
There is a definite kind of person who can be described as an addictive personality. Contrary to popular opinion, addiction is a problem for all ages, not just younger people. Addictive people cannot resist certain things which seem to gain such a hold on them that they cannot live without them. The most common addiction is alcoholism, but today there is also a wide addiction to other drugs as different from each other as heroin and glue. The kind of drug an addict chooses tends to be one that is easiest to obtain and socially acceptable to peer groups. In its wider sense the addictive personality can also become hooked on gambling in its various forms, and even on computers and television.

The psychology of addictive personalities has several traits. They are people who have grand illusions. They tend to think big and actually achieve very little. They are devious and become masters of self-deception. I was once asked to see a man dying in hospital from alcohol poisoning. He, however, insisted that it was his smoking that was a problem, and died maintaining this.

The only real cure for addicts is to get them right off their particular choice of addictive substance. In one sense they are never cured, but are people who have come to an honest recognition that alcohol, or whatever, has such a hold on them that they are helpless at controlling it, and need a power outside themselves and greater than themselves to do so. The control they must exercise is to abstain completely, for which they need the help of a group together with a trust in God, or as Alcoholics Anonymous says, 'A greater power than themselves'.

Because of the cleverness of addicts in covering up, they are often very difficult to recognise in the early stages. They do however very soon begin to have a bad effect on their families. Debt is the main one. Somehow or other the money that should be spent on other things disappears. If the addict is a parent this is usually the main way in which harm is done, because children will go without necessary things; whenever children appear neglected some kind of addictive problem should be suspected. Men who are addicts tend to become moody and violent, beating wives and children. Women can become violent but usually have the appearance of being inadequate, neglecting the home and children. Addictive teenagers tend to become withdrawn and evasive as well as moody. They often steal money, and in many cases teenage drug addiction has become a major cause of petty theft and burglary.

There are many people who use all kinds of drugs but do not become addicted because they do not have addictive personalities. It also seems that addiction can be slowly learned, and there is some evidence that bad social conditions and other psychological problems can encourage addiction, the main one being lack of genuine loving supportive relationships. This last a helper can provide, but on its own it is not enough. The addict **must** get group help from those who specialise in giving it, for example Alcoholics Anonymous. Support groups should also be found for the families so that they can learn the best way to relate to their addictive member. Family support groups are even more important when the addict will not admit to the addiction.

(ii) Problems involving children and adolescents

Child abuse, cruelty and neglect in their various forms are increasingly coming to light. Only rarely are the adults involved actually wicked and uncaring. Child abusers are in most cases inadequate or themselves overburdened with problems that are beyond them.

In the main, this area is covered by the NSPCC who should be contacted in most cases. The society is not just an agency concerned with prosecuting those who are cruel to children, although it does do so when appropriate. Its main concern is with improving care and therefore it is happy to give help and advice. A helper should therefore feel free to contact this nationwide agency even on the faintest suspicion of a problem because it better to be mistaken, than to miss out on something that could be nipped in the bud by involving someone equipped to do a proper investigation of the suspected problem family.

Another area of child abuse is incest and sexual abuse. This is now regularly in the news and considered by many as a 'vice of our times'. However, it may simply be that it is now more exposed than it was, mainly by the media. In the past fifteen years I have counselled a steady stream of people who were victims of incest, all ages and from all strata of society. It is a very serious and hurtful problem that affects the whole of a person's adult life if it is not dealt with. Often the process begins with a confidence shared with a very trusted friend, the helper, who can then refer the case for expert help. Probing motivated by curiosity will not help in discussing cases of incest and sexual abuse.

A very wide area of problems are to do with the children's education. Slow learners, dyslexic children, and also gifted children whose difference is not understood by the rest of the family all need help from various specialist agencies and individuals. The helper can usually recognise the problem by overt activities such as stealing, truancy, and bad social behaviour, all of which has a degree of protest. In extreme cases some sensitive children become depressed, withdrawn and suicidal. These problems are found all across the social groupings. Bed wetting usually indicates an insecurity which is difficult to pinpoint but does not necessarily point to a need for any expert to get involved.

The final area of widespread concern here is the lone parent family. The main problem in development for the child is the lack of modelling caused by the absence of a person of the opposite sex to the lone parent. There are also economic hardships as well, but group support is important in such cases, as well as a helper who can become a trusted confidant for the custodial parent.

(iii) Elderly relatives
The main problems with elderly relatives are: firstly that they do not always fit into families and can cause harm to young children's development; and secondly that they sometimes need specialist care, usually medical, which cannot be given by caring relations. Both of these problems cause feelings of guilt, hostility, despair and hopelessness within the caring relatives. These feelings can lead to tensions within the family for which a professional counsellor's help is required.

Counselling in these situations is very complex. In most cases it is the supporting relatives who need it more than the elderly person. I think it is true to say that people who do not face up to their 'hang-ups' when young, and come to terms with them, will inevitably grow into miserable, bitter and impossible to live with old people. They will also pass on these negative emotions to the next generation who are parents at this stage. Young children will then pick up the tensions and become 'anti' the elderly, seeing them as miserable, self-centred kill-joys. I have dealt with a considerable number of cases of bed wetting children, which ceased when an elderly cantankerous relative for whom the family were caring went to live elsewhere. However, the parent of the child who was also a child, nephew or niece of the elderly person needed hours of counselling to sort out the knock-on effects of their relationship with the elderly person, which often originated in their childhood.

The elderly must be cared for and helped to die with dignity, but we must be realistic about this because old people are like the rest of us, a mixture of good and bad. Many are almost impossible to live with, but on the other hand, many are a delight to know. The old need the young and a certain amount of exposure to them, and there are many positive relationships between old and young people from which both have benefited.

Having said this, however, the elderly need a degree of separation from the young because the environment they need in which to feel secure and happy is so different. The elderly need peace and quiet, the young are naturally exuberant and noisy. Too much of this will tire the elderly. Old people live in their past and tend to reflect on it, the young need to live in the present with an eye to the future. The elderly need to prepare themselves for death in a positive way, the young for their future, and so on. Preparation for death and learning to die with dignity is a most important issue. There has for years been an avoidance of this but *only those who have learned to come to terms with death can fully live.*

Spiritual help in this area is most important and the hospice movement is making a great contribution here. Although not all who die are old, most are. The helper needs to be familiar with the local hospice movement and churches as an essential part of their support of the elderly, as well as other groups that give support and care in this field. This includes medical care for pain relief, so that the life that remains in this world can be lived out with dignity and quality.

(iv) Problems within the marriage relationship

In all families a stable relationship between the parents is obviously very important. Firstly because it gives stability for the whole family, and secondly because it gives good modelling for the young in male/female relationships which is vital for their nurture into mature adulthood. A helper trusted by one or both partners is in a very positive position here, but must be wise enough not to become involved too deeply when tensions arise between them because this is the point where professional help is needed.

Professional help in marriage problems is necessary for two reasons. Firstly, it protects the relationship that the helper already has with the couple so that it can continue to be supportive in the future. In conflicts, the helper can be drawn to, or appear to be drawn to, one side or the other and get blamed and scapegoated by the couple, and sometimes totally rejected.

Secondly, marriage conflicts tend to require specialist help, and the training for this alters the relationship between the couple and their counsellor/helper in such a way that the professional counsellor/helper cannot have a friend/confidant kind of relationship. As the friend/confidant relationship is of value in itself and is the one that the non-professional helper is best equipped to give, it is important to protect it by handing over to the specialist marriage guidance counsellor all issues involving conflict and tension between the couple as they arise. No harm can be done by advising couples to seek help from experts when they do not really need it, but much damage can be done when a helper who is a well established friend/confidant, tries to help by getting involved in conflicts as a mediator.

Helpers also need to be aware that not all marriage relationship problems can be helped by marriage guidance counselling. Marriage guidance is about improving existing relationships. In cases where there is deep psychological disturbance in one of the partners, or even less severe problems, expert help for the individual needs to be sought, because in such cases marriage counselling cannot be effective. Marriage guidance counsellors will recognise when this situation exists and direct the individual concerned to appropriate help.

To conclude, the non-professional helper must always seek to maintain his or her role as personal friend/confidant of the couple, and because of the complex nature of the marriage relationship, always advise them to seek expert help where conflicts and tensions arise between them.

(v) Mental illness in families

The main problem the helper has in this area will be in recognising mental illness. Bizarre behaviour is always very frightening for those who have to live with it. This means that panic and over-reaction to them is the usual response, and any helper will get caught up in this. The practical outcome tends to be, 'They are mad, put them away where we will all be safe'. This is understandable because in some cases mentally ill people are a danger both to themselves and others. The most common label given to such people is 'schizophrenic' but a helper must be aware that bizarre behaviour such as hearing voices does not of itself mean that a person is having an attack of schizophrenia although it is one of the symptoms of such an attack. It is important that the helper has some idea of the difference between psychotic and neurotic behaviour. Eccentric people are usually neurotic and do not need psychiatric treatment. Skilled counselling can help them if they will accept it, and with a little understanding, practical wisdom and tolerance they can be lived with. The neurotic has not lost contact with reality. They may see it in a distorted way, but they have not lost contact and still have reflective powers so that a person they trust can reason with them. This is not so with psychotic illness. The power to reason with others is gone, they have lost contact with what most people recognise as 'the real world' and there is no point of contact from which a reasonable relationship can be made with them. These attacks may not last long, but when a person is in a psychotic state they need protection from themselves and other people need protection from them, because they can become violent. These factors point to the need for psychiatric help in such cases. Having sought this the helper's main task is to support the rest of the family while the crisis lasts.

Under adverse conditions, some neurotic people can go into a psychotic state. The difference between psychosis and neurosis is not a rigid one, and neither is the division between normality and neurosis. The normal person is hard to define because we all tend to relate normality to how we as individuals perceive others and the world around us. Perhaps the best test of serious mental illness is the inability to communicate with other people because the terms of reference used for that purpose are so bizarre that there is no common ground for understanding anything. Because of this the seriously mentally ill person is living in his or her fantasy world; a world that is meaningless to others who are living in a world with plenty of shared points of reference. This means that the rest of us would appear to be sharing a world in which the psychotic, or mentally ill person does not belong.

This, I think, is the essence of what is called 'mental illness'. It shows that it too has a high degree of relativity. Therefore we must all take care not to become too dogmatic in our definition lest we dehumanise such people in our own defence against the threat that their behaviour has to our idea of sanity. The practical issue seems to come back to, 'How do other people live with such a person and not go down under the strain?' The answer most societies have come up with is to find such people 'asylum', then both the 'sane' and the 'insane' can live without threatening each other.

The following statement is a summary of the psychotic/neurotic issue that is useful for a helper to remember.

It has been said that while a neurotic builds castles in the sky, a psychotic moves into them. This witticism contains a kernel of truth. Although most people have difficulties, they can at least distinguish reality from unreality. The cardinal characteristic of a psychotic disturbance is that the individual cannot adequately make this distinction in some important realm of life. The psychotic person, as it were, lives in a world of their own.

(vi) Physically handicapped and chronically ill

There is little to say about this class of problem because they are easily recognised and cause much stress to families that have such a person to care for. The helper needs to see that the relevant help is sought from the agencies that are equipped to offer it.

(vii) Spiritual aspects of helping

There are two main areas in problems of spiritual experience in which a helper would need to consult experts. One is negative and the other is positive.

The negative aspect is when families or individual members have frightening supernatural experiences such as a haunted house, poltergeists, demonic possession and allied frightening phenomena. There is a tendency for people to try to explain these things away by the use of psychological and pseudo-scientific reasons. This is understandable because many can be explained in this way, such as flights of imagination that some people have and are so similar to some of the symptoms of psychotic illness that they can easily be mistaken as such. These negative supernatural phenomena do have a reality in themselves, and where they are suspected it is wise to get expert advice. Anglican and Roman Catholic Bishops do have people who can be consulted and who are able to give help. Their names can be found in the local diocesan year book or directory, or an approach might be made through the Bishops's secretary.

The helper needs to be careful not to rush in where angels fear to tread. A good deal of listening and questioning needs to take place. Many people whose problem is purely psychological claim to be possessed by the devil. Therefore this claim alone is not a sign of validity but needs further investigation. The most important line of enquiry is to find out if the complainant has been involved in seances, witchcraft, or any other occultist activity, or has had family members or close contact with others who have done so. Many people dabble in occultist practices without being harmed, but some become seriously hurt. Those who shun them and keep well away are unlikely to become affected. In all cases where the helper has any suspicion that the root of all the trouble is negative supernatural forces, expert help should be sought as soon as possible.

The positive side of spiritual problems is mainly to do with people seeking a meaning for their life, trying to come to terms with death, fear of non-existence, the future, and confusion about the evil in the world. These are not totally intellectual questions, but always have a large underlying emotional content and their resolution is basically spiritual in nature. Many kinds of reactive depression and anxiety states are not psychological or medical problems but theological and spiritual ones in essence. They are to do with a lack of trust and the experience of being loved that disables the sufferer and prevents them from perceiving a loving purpose lying beneath the overtly threatening and non-loving evils that the present world presents.

This complex kind of problem needs to be dealt with by someone who has both spiritual and psychological understanding. The temptation is always that the helpers get drawn into intellectual arguments over such issues. These are totally futile and must be avoided. Any such person asking these deep and agonising questions needs expert counselling over a long period of time because such people suffer much. Because their suffering cannot always be labelled easily by most professional helping disciplines, they are often seen as argumentative nuisances or disgruntled intellectuals whom most people shun. Such organisations as the Clinical Theology Association (St Mary's House, Church Westcote, Oxford, OX7 6SF) work in this area which involves the relationship between psychology and theology, and offers help through their seminars and conferences.

EPILOGUE

In order to tie up all the loose ends and draw this section to a satisfactory close, I intend in this short conclusion to underline what I believe to be the basis from which all help to families must be given. It is in one word – **Love**. Having said this, further qualification is necessary because of the many diverse ways in which we use this word in our general conversation. The word 'love' means many things to many people, some of the meanings appearing to be contradictory. I want to show why love is the *only* basis from which a helper can function with any degree of success.

The underlying theme that I have followed can be described in two words: 'Being' and 'Becoming'. This is the process of growth that all human beings follow. The family is the main agency for promoting and sustaining its growth in its early stages, setting up a pattern for the future development of personal growth. Therefore the family, and in particular the nuclear family, is not an end in itself but a means to an end, the end being the full maturity of the individual person in relationship to all other people, and indeed the whole of creation. Let me further summarise the being/becoming process.

Being

This is what we now are at any point in our life. The baby, when a baby, needs to be sustained as a baby and not expected to do things appropriate to an adult. It is within the context of a loving family that its needs are best met. The adult also needs to be sustained by good loving relationships appropriate to whatever stage of life he or she is at. Love and acceptance are key factors in this. They are expressed by others in words such as 'I think you are great, I love you just as you are'. Everyone needs this positive affirmation by some person or persons to sustain their being as a human person. Families provide this in babyhood and early childhood. However in adulthood this is not necessarily so, but in any case at all stages of our life a committed relationship which includes real understanding is vital to sustain our Being. It helps us to use our conflicts within the wider world as a means of growth and wholeness, rather then becoming a cause of despair which can lead to our personal disintegration.

Becoming

This term I have used to describe our growth into our full potential as a human being. It includes our gifts or talents, learning to love and be loved, having a dignity of our own which will give us grace to respect others and treat the world in which we live with respect. Finally to die, leaving this world with that measure of grace and dignity described by Paul in his second letter to Timothy:

> . . . the time of my departure has come. I have fought the good

fight, I have finished the race, I have kept the faith. Henceforth is laid up for me a crown of righteousness, which the Lord, the righteous judge, will award me on that day, and not only to me, but to all those who have loved his appearing.

(2 Timothy Chapter 4 verse 6)

Being and Becoming are equally important aspects of our growth. Well nurtured being without exposure to the harsher realities of the outside world is not only escapist, but also destructive of an individual's personal growth. The process of becoming our full selves and reaching maturity of character, not only requires sustenance that comes from a good nurture, but also adversity, so that by wrestling with it we grow strong and purposeful. It is essential that we get both in the correct balance. The absence or inadequacy of either is equally bad for the process of personal growth which I have called 'becoming'.

Means to an end
A good nuclear family is not an end in itself, but a means to an end. Many problems arise when the nuclear family is idealised, and the individual's growth may be crushed by it. Because, in such a situation, the frustration which individuals feel at not being able to be and to become themselves turns to hatred, the nuclear family is attacked as enemy number one.

As a counsellor I regret this, and have argued for the nuclear family to be valued and supported. The fact that because of educational neglect there are lots of bad nuclear families and people get hurt by belonging to them, does not of itself indicate that the nuclear family is a fundamentally flawed institution. Families are essential institutions for all of us, and in all cultures, but they must be seen and understood for what they are, namely a means for giving us all as individuals a good launch into life, no more and no less.

Having said this, I will end with what I believe to be the only basis from which people can be enabled to form nuclear families that will serve their true purpose. It is also the only basis from which helpers can work in supporting families.

It is learning to love and be loved which Sigmund Freud said was a true sign of human maturity. This is a long and painful process that is at the heart of what I have described in 'Being' and 'Becoming'. It is also basically a religious quest because it originates, as does the whole of creation and we ourselves, in God.

The most adequate description of love that I know of anywhere is the following quotation which I urge you to meditate on frequently. By so doing I believe you will be helped to become a better mother, father, brother, sister, friend or helper.

If I have all the eloquence of men or of angels, but speak without love, I am simply a gong booming or a cymbal clashing. If I have the gift of prophecy, understanding all the mysteries there are, and knowing everything, and if I have faith in all its fullness, to move mountains, but without love, I am nothing at all. If I give away all I possess, piece by piece, and if I even let them take my body to burn it, but am without love, it will do me no good whatever.

Love is always patient and kind; it is never jealous; love is never boastful or conceited; it is never rude or selfish; it does not take offence, and it is not resentful. Love takes no pleasure in other people's sins but delights in the truth; it is always ready to excuse, to trust, to hope and endure whatever comes.

Love does not come to an end. But if there are gifts of prophecy, the time will come when they must fail; or the gift of languages, it will not continue for ever; and knowledge – for this, too, the time will come when it will fail. For our knowledge and our prophesying is imperfect; but once perfection comes, all imperfect things will disappear. When I was a child, I used to talk like a child, and think like a child and argue like a child, but now I am a man, all childish ways are put behind me. Now we are seeing a dim reflection in a mirror; but then we shall be seeing face to face. The knowledge that I have now is imperfect; but then I shall know as fully as I am known.

In short, there are three things that last: faith, hope and love; and the greatest of these is love.

(Paul's first letter to the Corinthians, Chapter 13).

Part Three

Small Groups for Spiritual and Emotional Growth

Chapter VII

Setting the Small Group within its Context

Society in the Western world today is in a state of rapid change which involves much breakdown of family life, and with this a lack of supportive relationships. Many people are lonely and unsupported emotionally and spiritually, so that they are unable to work out very important issues to do with their own personal lives and growth. This leaves them frustrated with a feeling that there is more to life than they are aware of, but without any means of discovering this extra dimension. The most positive way this frustration is expressed is in a desire to be really human.

Secular therapies are seeking ways to meet this need, but the Church needs to point out that to be truly human is only possible when the Divine is fully recognised. In his book *The Orthodox Way*, Fr Kallistos Ware shows how materialism and denying or demeaning God and the spiritual dimension of life diminishes, and at times, cruelly represses human beings. He concludes that, 'The only secure basis for a doctrine of human liberty and human dignity is the belief that each man is in God's image' (*The Orthodox Way*, p67 Mowbrays 1979).

With this in mind, I aim to give those who feel called to lead small groups – especially for spiritual and emotional growth – something to guide them. Since the issues are complex, I hope to reduce them to something worthwhile that is of practical value. Enough information will be contained here for those who do not wish to read further, but there is also a bibliography at the end of the book for those who do. My method is to bring together the work done on groups outside the Church and a Christian Theology of growth of the person, then to show the place of groups in the process of growth. All the techniques and insights of secular group dynamics are valid for the Christian group leader if they are based on accurate observation. The whole world is God's creation, and when Jesus Christ entered it, He put God's seal of approval on human life. All accurate observations and insights based on them are of God, even if the observer claims to be an atheist. The danger of the secular approach lies firstly, in inaccurate observation, and secondly, in making the insight or technique derived from such observations, a basis for a philosophy of life that becomes idolatry. St Paul saw this clearly. In his letter to the Romans he writes 'They exchanged the truth about God for a lie and worshipped and served the creature rather than the creator' (Romans Chapter 1 verse 25).

If then, secular techniques can be used by Christian group leaders and seen as valid, how do we avoid the danger of Pantheistic Paganism as shown by St Paul? The answer would seem to lie in an accurate understanding of both the sacred and the secular. To make everything sacred (ie spiritual) will deny the reality of much of the world in which we live. To deny the sacred (ie the place of God who is 'other than' the material world) is to fix us in a very narrow confine and dehumanise everything.

Charles Davis, in his book, *God's Grace in History* would seem to put his finger on the issues involved when he says:

> Secularism is a narrowing of human consciousness, a refusal to accept the tensions inherent in a complex and balanced mentality. The problem of balance in complexity is solved by suppressing the sacred. The Christian cannot reply by repressing the secular. He has the more difficult task of respecting the two sides of the distinction, both in theory and in his own life.
> (The Maurice Lectures 1996 p36, Collins Library of Theology and Philosophy).

The answer lies in God's grace on which the group leader must rely. Grace is God's free giving of himself to all people, it is an 'unconditional love'. It involves the sacred entering into the secular (Incarnation), because this is the very nature of Christ. God will not force himself upon his own creation; the secular has an autonomy of its own which God respects, but his grace to us is always available.

For group leaders, being a Christian is vital, not just having theories about God or Jesus at an intellectual level, but allowing Jesus to make us a new creation by the operation of the Holy Spirit within us. St Paul in his letter to the Corinthians says, 'If anyone is in Christ, he is a new creation' (2 Corinthians Chapter 5 verse 17). This does not happen to us as quickly as we think. The old Adam takes a long time to die and must be reckoned with. Being a Christian involves spiritual disciplines based on obedience to Christ in the Church and fellowship with others that will promote growth. As the Christian grows in Christ, he develops a greater self-awareness and also becomes more open to the Holy Spirit who is available as a resource for spiritual and emotional growth. Groups should provide a supporting milieu in which this can happen. Families alone do not provide this and in the modern world faith is impaired through isolation from others who can demonstrate the love of God by an unconditional acceptance of us as individuals.

When considering the place and nature of groups, it is essential to realise their importance for our very being. Nobody can exist as a human being without belonging to some group or other. This tends to happen in such a way that we do not always realise it.

In the book of Genesis we read, 'It is not good for man to be alone' (Genesis Chapter 2 verse 18), which states plainly that we all need other people, and this is where groups of one sort or another begin, in our very nature and its basic needs. When a person becomes totally isolated from others, the sense of personal identity becomes confused and eventually lost. It is for this reason that solitary confinement is used in prisons as punishment, but especially so for political reasons in states ruled by tyrants. By such isolation individuals' identities can be broken so that they are prepared for political re-education, in order that their deviance from accepted group behaviour can be corrected.

The importance of groups can also be seen by observing how people who are free to choose what they do, tend automatically to drift into groups. C S Lewis, in his book *Screwtape Proposes a Toast* (p 28, Fontana, Collins) begins the chapter 'The Inner Ring' with the following quotation from Tolstoy.

When Boris entered the room, Prince Andrey was listening to an old general, wearing his decorations, who was reporting something to Prince Andrey, with an expression of soldierly civility on his purple face. 'Alright. Please wait!' he said to the general, speaking in Russian with the French accent which he used when he spoke with contempt. The moment he noticed Boris he stopped listening to the general who trotted imploringly after him and begged to be heard, while Prince Andrey turned to Boris with a cheerful smile and a nod of the head. Boris now clearly understood – what he had already guessed – that side by side with the system of discipline and subordination which were laid down in the Army Regulation, there existed a different and more real system – the system which compelled a tightly laced general with a purple face to wait respectfully for his turn while a mere captain like Prince Andrey chatted with a mere second lieutenant like Boris. Boris decided at once that he would be guided not by the official system but by this other unwritten system (*War and Peace*, part III chapter 9).

This shows something which with a little reflection we can probably all recall if we have spent time within any kind of institution. Namely, within the normally accepted structures, small in-groups always form. C S Lewis called it the 'inner ring', but whatever we may call it, whether we may like it or not, such things are inevitable because they arise out of our human nature and its emotional needs. If then, such things are there, we would be wise not to wish they were not, or try to organise them in a better way; but seek to understand them, and by so doing work with them. Because, as we have already said, they arise out of our very nature, we are dealing with something the roots of which are far deeper than is usually seen by superficial observation. In this chapter therefore, the different types of groups to which people automatically belong during their lifetime will be described, together with the emotional needs that these groups supply. The purpose of this is to set the small group within its correct context before going on to deal with our main topic – small groups and their leadership.

It can be roughly categorised that every one of us belongs to three different types of groupings. We may not realise it until we reflect on our lives, but every time we have an organised group – a church group, or any other sort of group – we have to understand the patterns of groupings that there are, and not work against them. If we have false expectations and work against the nature of the group, we will create problems. Groups that are bad groups, have problems and do not work mainly because people have tried to make the group do what it cannot do.

In his book, *Everyday God* (Birmingham University, Chapter 12) J G Davies points this out. He carefully describes the three different types of group. These three different types, known as Primary, Secondary and Tertiary groups, will now be described and illustrated. First, tertiary groups.

A tertiary group is a group that is very large. It gives a person an underlying sense of identity. It demands no real personal commitment because it is a group one belongs to almost by accident, just by being alive and being born into a certain situation. Examples of tertiary groups are: being British, being Catholic, being Protestant, being Baptist, being Anglican, being Conservative, being Labour . . . It is large groups of this kind which demand very low commitment levels most of the time, that determine what is a tertiary group. Sometimes there is a commitment to it and sometimes there is not. It is a group to which people just belong and only feel strongly about in terms of commitment when certain needs arise.

The key tertiary group is nationality. People can get problems which are not recognised unless one knows about the nature of groupings. An example of this is a man in his mid forties who was depressed, tearful and uncertain. Nobody really knew what was wrong with him until he ended up in a counselling centre. It took about a year to find out, and after many hours of talking and probing, the key issue was found to be this. His father and mother moved to Australia where he was born, and he grew up there until he was twenty-one but his parents never sorted out the question of nationality. Eventually the parents died and he came to England where he found a job and settled down. When he was about forty he wanted a passport to go somewhere on business, and this was the time his depression began. He found that he could not have one because he did not have British nationality, and Australia would not give him one because he never had Australian citizenship. This made him feel, in his own words 'a nothing'. This case adequately illustrates the purpose of the tertiary group. It is mainly to give us an identity. We belong to this group of people, and because it does not demand too much commitment, the fact that a person belongs to it could go unnoticed for years until something like the case above crops up. Because our basic need is for it to be there at all times, we only tend to become aware of it when for some reason it does not seem to be there. Stateless people become acutely aware of this, while those who live in undisturbed and stable countries wonder what the stateless are fussing about. Such is the nature of tertiary groups.

The secondary group is a group consisting of anything from about fifteen to twenty, maybe up to about a hundred or two hundred people; it could even possibly go up to five hundred. It is not numbers that are most important for such a group, it is the type of function that it performs for the person. The definition of a secondary group is that it is a group in which intimacy at any deep level cannot take place because it is too big, and yet the people in the group know each other at a superficial level. In a tertiary group, knowledge of the other people in the group – that is, personal knowledge gained through a personal relationship – is totally irrelevant. In a secondary group, a person's name, face and other such details are recognised and known. When a secondary group becomes larger it is not possible to know everybody's name, but it is possible to say 'That is the man or lady who does this or that within our group'.

The qualities of the secondary group are that they actually sustain the individual within it without threatening to expose too much of a personal nature to other people within the group. Let me give you some examples of secondary groups. The most common examples are from places of work, an office is one. There could be fifteen or twenty or thirty people working in an office which functions socially by having ceremonies like Christmas parties or leaving parties, involving collections to give presents. They can be quite informal family-type groups, but as they get bigger they become much more institutionalized; for example, a comprehensive school of about twelve hundred pupils and a staff of sixty. This would be a quite involved type of secondary group, with subgroups of a secondary nature within it. Another type of secondary group is a church congregation which is the local worshipping community as opposed to the general tertiary groups, (eg Anglicans, Methodists etc). This can be as few as ten or eleven people, and it can function at this size as a secondary group, because those ten or eleven people do not relate very intimately, and yet they do know each other reasonably well. Of other secondary groups, we can look at a factory, college, university department or any group that involves people working together, where the purpose, size and relationship between them fits the secondary group definition.

The other main quality of a secondary group, which is important, is that it is pretty stable. It is true that firms, schools and colleges close down, and when they do there is quite a bit of trauma, but people very soon find themselves another secondary group to which to attach themselves. The relevant point is that it is a group we can leave and it still functions; for example, if we are on holiday and do not go to church for a month, the church worship still goes on. If we leave the office and have a holiday for two or three weeks, the office still goes on. The comprehensive school still goes on when some of the pupils or some of the teachers are absent because its basic function and nature are not fundamentally changed by individual absences.

Another feature of secondary groups is organisation. They must have some degree of organisation to function, and because of this they provide a hierarchy of jobs, which, as a by-product, gives people status. The negative side of a secondary group is that it can be the basis of an awful lot of infighting which is destructive. This infighting, of course, can have a positive side which is stimulating for personal growth, but it does not stimulate personal growth very much. The tensions of a large group tend to result in political jockeying for status, and in this situation some people can be pushed to the wall, whereas the strong survive. So some can use the secondary group to work out all sorts of things in themselves which are to do with status and power, whereas other people are very vulnerable in it, but even the vulnerable can find a place to hide so that they are not overwhelmed.

Finally, the secondary group has a specific function; a school for teaching, an office for doing certain types of work, a factory for producing goods. Purpose is much more important in a secondary group than it is in the tertiary group, but the purpose is not individual-centred. The individual cannot have everything centred on himself or herself in a secondary group. What they get out of it is not obvious, because the central aim of the secondary group is to fulfil some purpose other than the individual's interest, and yet, in an indirect way, the individual's interests do seem to be met to some degree. It is this clash between the individual's interests and the interests of the secondary group that causes a great deal of the friction and political jockeying that goes on in such groups.

So then, let us sum up the qualities of a secondary group.

(i) They offer us a chance to know and be known at a not very deep and threatening level, but at a level that can sustain us considerably.

(ii) They do not depend entirely on our presence. They can keep going without us. Our absence from the group is noticed and regretted, or in some cases people will note with joy that the painful man in the third desk from the right has gone. But nevertheless they can carry on without us.

(iii) They can carry us. The secondary group can carry us when we are not up to scratch and not putting anything into it. It can keep on going without us, and thus give us a sense of status and support.

In conclusion we can see that the secondary group has a very important role to play in the needs of the individual, even though as a group it is not set up to be individual centred. The individual's gain from the group is a by-product of the group's main function, which is to do something which is centred away from individual people, for example, in a church worship, in a factory making whatever the factory makes, in an office doing the work, in a school teaching, etc. The secondary group does not supply great intimacy and intimate needs, and in fact people can be carried along by a secondary group who are very bad at making personal relationships. Some people can actively use the group as a means of avoiding painful relationships. It also gives stability and purpose to everyone and it is a group to which we all need to belong. Some of us can belong to two secondary groups. We can, for example, belong to a certain industry that employs us in the week and also to something like a golf club or tennis club, or any type of club that functions at weekends. This could include membership of a church as well. Therefore there are work secondary groups and also pleasure or recreational secondary groups, all of which are of equal importance to us.

It is because secondary groups do not provide the intimacy and stimulus which individuals need to be fully human that inevitably within them 'inner rings' form, as C S Lewis demonstrated by referring to the writings of Tolstoy, quoted at the beginning of this chapter. The 'inner ring', is of course, the primary group to which we will now direct our attention.

A primary group is a group that is very small, and consists of about ten or twelve people. It could be as small as six or eight and could be stretched up to about fourteen or fifteen. The positive nature and value of a primary group is that it is a group within which very intimate relationships can develop. It is a group in which individuals can work out their problems, can learn to experience love and acceptance, and thereby be encouraged and strengthened, to face the stresses and strains of life. It is also a group which can be very creative. From such groups can come all sorts of ideas that can be fed into a secondary group to bring about changes in it, because as we have said, one of the qualities of a secondary group is its stability. This stability can be stifling, so it therefore needs the stimulus generated by a primary group that is in some way related to it. Peter Berger makes reference to this stimulus that comes from a small group in the first chapter of his book *A Rumour of Angels* (pp 18-21). He calls such a group a 'Cognitive Minority Group' because it can be a group of people who hold very strong beliefs that are not those of the majority, and yet they are able to influence the whole of society. In the case of the Christian faith, it is interesting to note that what eventually became a world wide movement began with Jesus Christ and the twelve apostles, an example of a primary group that could also be described as a cognitive minority group.

So therefore we can see that the positive side of a primary group is firstly, that it can benefit individuals by being a place in which they can grow, experience love and work out problems; and secondly, it can be valuable in that it is a place of ideas and dynamism from which people can move out to have an effect on larger groups and society as a whole. The negative side of the primary group can be summed up simply in that it has no lasting power. It is quite natural for a primary group to come into being, function at a specific task for a certain period of time, and eventually die or disintegrate. Some primary groups can be so full of dynamic interactions that they actually blow themselves to pieces and disintegrate rather more quickly.

There is only one thing that will keep a primary group going for longer than a year or eighteen months, or at the most, two years. It is when it ceases to function as a primary group and takes on the role of a secondary group. When this happens the whole thing stagnates and one might just as well have a secondary group and forget about it as a primary group.

It is for this reason that we have described tertiary and secondary groups, because a primary group can only be of value when it is related to a secondary group. A secondary group can contain people at a level that is safe and comfortable in between the collapses and endings of primary groups. In the church scene, for example, people who are in need of working out some point of faith can join a group for Lent or for some other limited period. This can be very beneficial for them, but it is also extremely demanding. Because of this fact, when they have worked out what they need to in the primary group, they can go back into the worshipping group, ie the congregation, which is the secondary group, and stay there until such time as they feel the need for further primary group activity to work on some other aspect of growth.

The best example of a primary group, as we have seen in Chapter IV, is the family. We cannot make every primary group like a family, but there are many people who benefit from them because they do not have a family which can enable them in their growth as persons.

Today, there is a need for primary groups, because there are many people who require this help. They are mostly people who have been deprived of a natural family that is spiritually and emotionally healthy. Perhaps people who have had good natural nuclear families do not need a primary group to the same degree. It is important to avoid forcing people into primary groups whether they like it or not. There has to be a need for people to be in a primary group, which they themselves acknowledge, for it to be a valid thing. Therefore individuals must have a reasonable degree of freedom to decide whether or not to join a primary group.

Shall we then conclude this chapter by saying a couple of important things? Firstly, if we are aware of tertiary, secondary and primary groups and their place and function, then we will not get confused about where we are and expect things that cannot be.

Secondly, because the main task of this section is to deal with the practical running of primary groups, from now on we are going to concentrate on this area. We must always, as we have said, refer back to the secondary and tertiary groups from time to time, because we cannot make a primary group anything other than a primary group. The purpose of this chapter has been to outline its place in the whole system of things: its strengths, its weaknesses and its limitations.

Chapter VIII

The Primary Group

The aim of this chapter is to outline the main characteristics of the primary group and to lay down some important principles to be observed by those responsible for setting up such groups. As there are many types of primary groups, we will concern ourselves with a general approach dealing with those things that apply across the board to any group falling within the broadest definition of being 'Primary'. The only qualification of this broad approach will be that what is said will be directed towards primary groups that are set up or specifically organised and not ones that develop spontaneously within secondary groups because of the nature of human beings and their needs.

The first characteristic that is important concerns size. A primary group will never tick as a primary group if there are more than twelve people in it. If it is larger than this, it ceases to be a primary group because people cannot relate to each other in the deep way that is required to make it a primary group. It can be as small as four or five, but if it is very small, people may not feel happy enough to open up in a deep way because there is the threat that members will feel that they have always got to do something, say something or be open to other people or else the group will not work. In a very small group it is impossible to hide feelings successfully. If one person is having an off day and leaving the others to get on with things, a group that is too small is quickly threatened. A very small primary group can be excessively threatening and very demanding of energy, and therefore likely to burn itself out quickly. Ten or twelve is best because if it is properly led and handled, individuals who want to have a little rest and be carried along, from time to time, can do so without actually being threatened or threatening to the life of the group. Therefore ten or twelve is probably the ideal.

There is, however, a problem which needs to be borne in mind. It is possible to have a primary group of twelve (the right number) but if it is not properly understood and led, it can actually develop into a secondary group with relationships becoming distant. This becomes apparent when people are afraid of opening up and speaking to each other, but just listen, so that the true feelings of individuals are hidden from each other and underlying individual agendas develop. These individual agendas will be discussed later, but they can be very very dangerous to the group's life, and if they are not recognised and brought out into the open, some clever and manipulative people will use them in such a way that they will destroy the group as a primary group. This is mentioned at this point to illustrate that although the correct size of the group is a *sine qua non* for correct functioning, even when this factor is right, it does not guarantee the success of the group as a primary group. Nevertheless it is a vital starting point because if this is not right to begin with, all other efforts will fail.

The second point about a primary group is that it must have a definite purpose that is understood and accepted by all the members. This means that if it is for example, a business group like a committee or council, whose purpose is to run the business affairs of a church, its purpose must be stated clearly and understood by all its members. It must be seen as a primary group in a well defined and specific relationship with its secondary group, the local congregation. This purpose must be clearly spelt out so that the council can aim to achieve what it was set up to do in a businesslike and efficient way. If this is not done, then the members become frustrated and at cross purposes with each other, thereby causing what was intended to become a decision-making group to become indecisive and inefficient. Here we have an example of the relationship between size and purpose. In many cases church councils allow themselves to deteriorate into a secondary group by co-opting too many members, not having proper elections or just by drifting into an ill-defined secondary group for fear of offending some who have served on it for years and ought to resign. To guard against this, Church councils ought to try to keep themselves small enough to remain primary groups and so retain their purpose. In large congregations where representation requirements make it impossible to keep the elected council down to primary group size, the best way of ensuring that the purpose of actually completing business is carried out, is to appoint sub-groups of primary size that have specific well defined tasks to carry out. In conclusion, any committee that has more than twelve members will never be able to work to a common purpose and make real decisions. A primary group is a very suitable decision making group, and we must therefore never let committees get too big or else decision making power is lost.

Another purpose for a group, in general terms, may be that of study. This also must be very specific about what it aims to study and keep to the point. If, for example, in a Bible study group, people start coming and wanting to pray about their problems, or if they start saying, 'Let us organise this or that, perhaps a coffee morning somewhere', members will object, saying, 'Hey, we have come here to study the Bible', and tensions will develop that could destroy the group. If on the other hand it is a prayer group, one has to be very careful about studying the Bible in it. It is not that the Bible must never be read, but the main aim must be spelled out and kept to, only referring to the Bible where it is obviously relevant to the main aim. Then there will not be conflicts and tensions that are destructive.

The third and final general type of group whose purpose is to be mentioned is one whose aim is to promote spiritual and emotional growth. This type of group will be looked at more fully in a later chapter, but one point about it needs to be mentioned here. These groups can best be described as those in which people learn to be open to each other, and in which there must be a very high level of trust, commitment and confidentiality, so that people can actually come and work out their spiritual and emotional hang-ups in an atmosphere that feels safe and supportive. This sort of group has to be very loving and accepting; people have to be allowed to talk rubbish for long enough for them to realise they are talking rubbish. This is a very important point, because if in this sort of group there is a person who is very corrective, and quotes the right text and right thing too quickly, people will just go into their shells and they will not come out with what they really feel or believe. Where there are deep hurts, confusions and false beliefs, people need to be given a few sessions to air their beliefs and come right out into the open. The group and leader just listen and question, thereby allowing them to work it all out for themselves. Eventually and prayerfully and at the right time it will become possible to help them to change, correct or develop what is thought or felt, but if anyone comes in too soon in a corrective manner, it will actually block them off, so that they will never learn and grow. This process is basically how spiritual growth comes, so if this is confused with say, a Bible study group, all sorts of chaos can develop. The usual way in which chaos develops is as follows: a specific book of the Bible might be being studied in the course of which someone comes up with something and goes on and on about it. The other people in the group resent this and sooner or later someone will say, 'Hey, let's get on with the text. We have come to study the text, we can't have all this going on!' This objection can harm the person going on and on by making them feel put down. It needs to be understood that people who do this sort of thing in study groups do so because they have underlying problems which are best dealt with in a group set up specifically for the purpose of spiritual and emotional growth, and not as a study group.

A primary group then, should have a definite limited purpose, and it must be worked out for each specific group. Therefore state very clearly that 'This group is . . . and we welcome people who wish to do this . . .' Groups always break up and cause all sorts of pain, gossip and trouble, when their purpose is not made clear.

The third point about the nature of a primary group is that it is an entity of itself with a distinct lifespan of its own. This must be recognised and worked with. So many primary groups die before they end because this has not been recognised; or is recognised, but ignored.

The time in chronological terms varies depending on a number of facts. If the group meets once a fortnight it will last longer than if it meets every evening. The governing factor with regard to lifespan would seem to be the working of the group agenda. All groups die as a group when the agenda is completed. To begin a new agenda is equivalent to starting a new group. The different agendas of its meetings are also vital in this respect. More will be said about this in the discussion of leadership.

There are, however, recognisable phases in the life of a group which need to be carefully noted and used as indicators of the stage a group is at with regard to its lifespan. They are as follows:

Phase one – the coming together of the group. This takes place as long as people are still learning to relate to one another in a meaningful way as demanded by the group's task. Members take note of what other people say, record things that ring bells for them and begin to work out how to respond to them. This is just human nature and the result is an inevitability of things happening inside individual members when a group first comes together. They express themselves in a variety of unspoken feelings which need working out. The following are typical examples: 'He is the vicar, we must watch what we say to him', or 'This is the local doctor, he knows things about me I have not told anyone else', or 'This is granny Jones and my family are in feud with her family because my grandpa said . . . therefore I must be careful what I say'.

All these individual agendas that people bring in the initial period of the group, are being worked out in a variety of ways. Therefore until they are worked out the group has not begun to operate according to its real purpose. And even if there are none of these strong agendas, which is most unlikely, there is an essential process of coming together that must take place at its own pace and in its own particular way for each group. People need time to be able to say, 'Yes, I am coming to know so and so, I am getting to like them, I am getting to understand them.'

Phase two – this is the main phase of the group's life and it is the time during which the work is done, be it Bible study, businesses, spiritual growth or anything else. People in groups tend to sense when this phase begins. It often expresses itself in the form of the following type awareness. One comes home one night from the group and is struck by the thought 'Goodness, these people are really loving each other and are relating! Things are happening, the group has come together'. This happy purposeful situation will only go on for a certain length of time with the work being done, and then the third phase of the group will begin in a similar way to that described in the beginning of the main phase. It is usual for one or two people to begin to feel that the group is not what it was. This is felt for a while before being voiced, and often the voicing creates a desire by some of the members to do something to save the group from decline. This kind of debate is nearly always symptomatic of the onset of phase three, the decline.

Phase three – the decline of the group really takes place when people begin to lose enthusiasm. They begin to make all sorts of funny excuses and absenteeism begins to grow. Some people begin to bring in other agenda, and all sorts of new tensions begin. For example, you may be in a Bible study group that has been studying Isaiah. You have had a good time and you have done very well and you have got to Isaiah 40, then suddenly someone comes in and says 'Do you know I saw a lesser spotted woodpecker running up my apple tree the other day?' 'Oh, that is interesting' comes the response and immediately everybody gets involved in talking about birds. A discussion starts and the leader who has been caught up in it suddenly thinks, 'Goodness, we have been at it half an hour and we have not even opened our Bibles'. Now this is a sign that people in the group have absorbed as much of Isaiah as they can take for the time being. We as human beings are like this. There is a natural level at which we can function and we can only give and take a certain amount in terms of spiritual, emotional and intellectual effort. Anyone who is sensitive to this can pick up the decline. The demands put on people by the life of the group can only be responded to in a positive way for a limited time, and this is why groups have a limited lifespan which must be accepted. As has already been mentioned, a primary group is an entity in itself comprising of individuals who enter into a network of inter-relationships peculiar to one specific group. The entry of a new person once phase two is reached is the entry of a foreign body, and the absence of a member is like the loss of a limb or organ. This is why absenteeism is such a powerful influence for decline. Individuals will automatically opt out or switch off when they have had enough. Nothing can be done to prevent this, and the resulting demise of the group, without denying the love and respect so essential as a basis for caring.

The fourth important aspect concerning a primary group is the nature of its leadership. All such groups must have a leader whose prime task is to enable the group to function and fulfil its purpose. The essential skills such a leader must have are ones that can discern the nature of the group's life, manage and direct that life in such a way that the energies and skills the group has, which are vested in individual members, are made available to the whole group. The leader must also have an authority recognised by all the members so that sufficient discipline can be asserted to see that the group's task is carried out. A good and easily memorised summary of this can be made using the letters **T. I. M.**

T. for task, **I.** for individual agenda, **M.** for maintenance of group unity.

Task – the group leader must thoroughly understand the task of the group, be able to spell it out clearly to every member in such a way that they understand it, and also ensure that the group does not drift away from it.

Individual agenda – every person in the group comes with his or her own agenda. The different agendas are important because they can be a source of energy which will make the group work, or a destructive energy that will destroy it. A good leader must be able to recognise this, and enable the agendas to find expression in the group in such a way that the creative parts can be utilized and the destructive parts neutralized.

There are three important points to remember that will help a leader to deal with individual agendas. The first one is to watch body language, especially facial expressions. This then allows certain questions to be asked that allow individual agendas to be expressed. For example, 'You look bored, George, are you fed up with what we are doing?' or 'Anne, you seem bursting with excitement, is this something you want to comment on?' or 'Alan, your hand has gone up and down several times, would you like to leave the room?!' The leader needs to observe, be sensitive and use humour in a relaxed way to bring out the agenda. The chief factor operating in regard to individual agendas is, 'Do people feel safe enough in the group to bring it out?' Therefore the leader must convey an air of safety through his or her own personality in the first place.

The second point is concerning silent, or, at least, less articulate group members. At every session it is important that the leader should involve them by asking a direct question such as, 'John, you have been quiet during this session, would you like to share any of your thoughts?' If John says 'No', this should be respected, but often less articulate people need to be helped into the group in this way and as a result contribute much that is of value and could easily be lost. This approach often stops resentment and a feeling of not belonging from developing within more silent members and thereby putting a block upon the growth and development of the group.

The final point about individual agendas is that the leader should make it a rule that every member is invited to contribute at every meeting. The leader should not feel obliged to answer all questions raised personally, but should often ask other group members to answer them, especially if he or she knows that they might have more expertise in certain areas. To do this is helpful in preventing an articulate member from taking the group over, especially if a dialogue can be started between such a member and one of an opposing view with the leader acting as referee. This can greatly help the leader to use the individual agendas of members creatively for the benefit of the whole group.

Maintenance of group unity – one important point already mentioned is that a primary group is an entity of itself with its own distinctive life. The role of the leader is to protect this entity. There are several ways in which this can be done. The first is to ensure that the membership is the same throughout. A new person joining or a person leaving after the group is formed can seriously damage its life. It can, *in extremis*, kill the group as a group. An agreed life expressed in terms of the number of meetings to which full commitment is expected must clearly be stated at the beginning.

The second important issue is that the leader must always be aware of the position of the group with regard to its lifespan. If it is already well into the decline stage before the agreed time or number of meetings is reached, then measures should be taken to end it early. If, on the other hand, it is late at arriving at this stage, then measures should be taken to extend the number of meetings. It is a good thing to have an assistant leader who is good at picking up the vibes that are important, and people who can do this cannot always lead. This issue will be discussed further in the chapter on leadership.

Finally, the leader must enable the group to make decisions about ending or continuing and anything else vital to its life. This is done by bringing all the different individual agendas that are relevant out into the open. If the leader makes a decision without doing this, and just informs the group, trouble will soon start. This is not simply government by a democratic majority, it is focusing the group's thoughts and feelings in such a way that they see the leadership's decisions as being in harmony with their own needs and desires.

Enough has been said about leadership for the time being. The point intended to be made now is that a primary group must have a leader and the leader must pay attention to certain things that are of the very nature of a primary group. For the leader to have the required authority and if the group is to have a specific purpose, he or she must be appointed by an outside authority and not just thrown up by the interaction of the group.

In concluding this chapter, a brief comment will be made about the spiritual aspect of primary groups. This will be taken up in more detail later. The comment has two parts – one is historical, and it is simply that in the history of the church, primary groups have been important in times of growth and spiritual renewal. The other is theological and it is that such groups can also be seen as a means of grace.

At the beginning of the Christian church, Our Lord developed the spiritual life and the emotional growth of the apostles in a primary group. St Augustine of Hippo in his early Christian life worked a lot out in a primary group consisting of his close friends in Cassiciacum. References to the emotional outworkings of this experience are recorded in the following passage from his 'Confessions' (*Confessions of St Augustine, book IX* p186).

How I cried out to you, my God, when I read the Psalms of David, those hymns of faith, those songs of a pious heart in which the spirit of pride can find no place. I was new to your true love. I was a catechumen living at leisure in that country house with Alypius, a catechumen like myself and my mother, who never left us. She had the weak body of a woman, but the strong faith of a man, the composure of her years, a mother's love for her son, and the devotion of a Christian. How I cried out to you when I read those Psalms! How they set me on fire with love of you! I was so burning to echo them to all the world, if only I could, so that they might vanquish man's pride. And indeed they are sung throughout the world, and just as none can hide away from the sun 'none can escape your burning heat' (Psalm 18 verse 7). The thought of the Manichees filled me with angry resentment and bitter sorrow, yet I pitied them too, because in their ignorance of the sacraments that heal us they raved against the very remedy that could have cured them of their madness. I wished that they could have been somewhere at hand, unknown to me, to watch my face and hear my voice as I read the fourth Psalm. They would have seen how deeply it moved me. 'When I call on your name, listen to me, O God, and grant redress; still, in time of trouble, you have brought me relief; have pity on me now, and hear my prayer' (Psalm 4 verse 2).

St Teresa of Avila also sought the renewal of her community through small groups; and John Wesley used small groups as a means of spiritual growth in the eighteenth century Methodist renewal in England.

As a means of grace the primary group has a very definite role to play. Grace could be defined as follows: 'The self-communication of God to his creatures' (Sacramentum Mundi 2, *An Encyclopedia of Theology*, Ed. Karl Rahner, p422, Burns and Oates 1968). A small group is a suitable place in which the specific outworking of grace, as defined above, can take place for the benefit of individuals, because grace is expressed by God's own self disclosure in love towards us. Its prime source is love not justice; therefore to be in touch with love, the prime source means a suspension of judgement for the time being. Justice is included, but God is just because he loves. This love of God can become a living experience for people in the context of a well run primary group, and for this reason it ceases to be just an academic theory. In order then to learn in the depth of our being the full meaning of grace, it has to be experienced through a combination of loving human relationships that also involve the self-disclosure of God. This is part of the mystery of the Incarnation that needs to become a living experience in the present moment for people to have a living faith. It is for this reason that a primary group can be an important means of grace at certain crucial periods of a person's life, as we shall see more fully in Chapter XII.

LEADERSHIP STYLE AND THE CHURCH

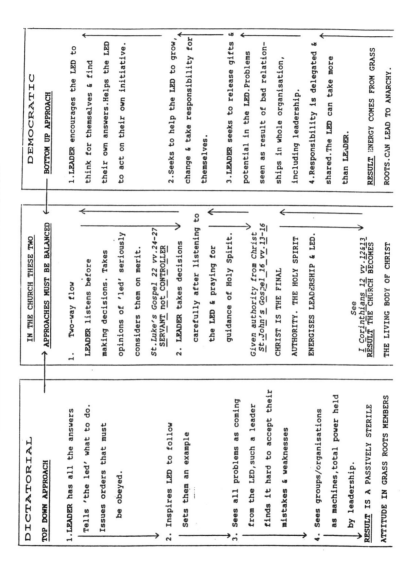

DICTATORIAL	IN THE CHURCH THESE TWO	DEMOCRATIC
TOP DOWN APPROACH	APPROACHES MUST BE BALANCED	BOTTOM UP APPROACH
1. LEADER has all the answers Tells 'the led' what to do. Issues orders that must be obeyed.	1. Two-way flow LEADER listens before making decisions. Takes opinions of 'led' seriously considers them on merit. *St.Luke's Gospel 22 vv.24-27* SERVANT not CONTROLLER	1. LEADER encourages the LED to think for themselves & find their own answers. Helps the LED to act on their own initiative.
2. Inspires LED to follow Sets them an example	2. LEADER takes decisions carefully after listening to the LED & praying for guidance of Holy Spirit. *Given authority from Christ St.John's Gospel 16 vv.13-16* CHRIST IS THE FINAL AUTHORITY. THE HOLY SPIRIT ENERGISES LEADERSHIP & LED.	2. Seeks to help the LED to grow, change & take responsibility for themselves.
3. Sees all problems as coming from the LED, such a leader finds it hard to accept their mistakes & weaknesses		3. LEADER seeks to release gifts & potential in the LED. Problems seen as result of bad relationships in whole organisation, including leadership.
4. Sees groups/organisations as machines, total power held by leadership.	*See I Corinthians 12 vv.12&13* RESULT THE CHURCH BECOMES THE LIVING BODY OF CHRIST	4. Responsibility is delegated & shared. The LED can take more than LEADER.
RESULT IS A PASSIVELY STERILE ATTITUDE IN GRASS ROOTS MEMBERS		RESULT ENERGY COMES FROM GRASS ROOTS. CAN LEAD TO ANARCHY.

Chapter IX

Styles of Leadership

In the previous chapter we have just seen how important leadership is for the correct functioning of a primary group. In this chapter, leadership will be examined with a view to discovering which style of leadership is best for a primary group, and why this is so. We are all limited by our own personality and for the purpose of leadership need to know our own strengths and weaknesses. This in turn will determine the kind of leadership style any individual will adopt, and whether or not that individual is suitable for primary group leadership. All forms of leadership are related to the situation in which leadership needs to be exercised and this always severely limits the number of suitable people for any specific kind of leadership. Small group leadership is no exception to this rule, indeed, it is most probably one for which only a few people are ideally suited, and therefore it is very important that group leaders should be chosen with considerable care if their activities are to be of any real and lasting value and disasters averted. The chart, 'Leadership Style and the Church' on p. 135 sets out the basic principles of all leaderships practised within a Christian context.

Over the centuries many attempts have been made to categorise personality types. Hippocrates, in classical Greece, put people into four categories – Sanguine, Choleric, Phlegmatic and Melancholic. This seems to be a basis from which many modern attempts have been developed. The modern discipline of psychology has refined these four and some have added types as a result. In addition, the more modern discipline of sociology, by the means of rigorous observation, has sought to understand styles of leadership within their social context. For our present purpose it is proposed that two approaches to understanding personality types will be examined, and also two styles of leadership so that the reader has some means of examining his or her potential for group leadership.

Of the personality types, we begin by looking at those defined by Dr Frank Lake in his book *Clinical Theology* (Chapter 2, Abridged Edition, 1986 DLT). The approach taken here is to do with a person's emotional responses to other people who are of importance to them in their development, especially in early years. It starts from a negative position, saying that deprivation of accepting love and/or emotional sustenance will cause a person to behave in a certain way towards others in order to obtain what is emotionally necessary for them to live as a person. We will look at this basic theory again in Chapter X in form of Frank Lake's 'Dynamic Cycle', but for the purpose of this chapter we will describe the five personality reaction types only in sufficient detail for them to be recognised by the reader in his or her own experience.

Before describing the five types of response, four important points must be made. Firstly, these types are fluid. As people grow spiritually and emotionally they change their type of response. Secondly, it is possible for us to have within us more than one of the types described. Thirdly, that the whole person is larger and more complex than the personality type response that will be described. Finally, it is important that for a full and really adequate understanding of these five types, people should participate in a Clinical Theology seminar, especially in the first year syllabus. The experience of a Clinical Theology seminar is important because it is in the group context that our true awareness is developed. That is why the Clinical Theology Association bases its training upon 'Seminar Group Experience'. Now let us look at the five types.

Firstly, the depressive type. This can best be described as the 'bottle it all up' person. Reactive depression is caused by the repression of feelings, and the depressive type person finds certain feelings so threatening that they tend to bottle them up, usually because of the fear of hurting others or getting 'out of control' themselves. Anger and anxiety are the most common feelings this type bottles up. This means that if such feelings are around in a group, they cannot cope with them. As such feelings are nearly always present in such groups this type of person will not make a group leader unless they get a lot of help in sorting themselves out. They tend to crush the life out of a group.

The second type is also a person who finds other people's feelings very threatening because of their own inner weakness. It is the paranoid personality type. Some people feel very weak within and fear being destroyed or overcome by other people's emotions. Their response is to take a very rigid legalistic and intellectual approach to other people's problems. They work everything by the book, love lots of rules and are most rigid and unbending. Informality and humour frighten them so much that it is obvious that they are most unsuitable for group leaders. Indeed, such people would hardly ever join a group and might just manage to read this without writing it off as nonsense.

Thirdly, we come to the anxiety state. This kind of person has a little in common with the paranoid in that they can become obsessive and rigid in an attempt to bring their anxiety under control, but most of the time the anxiety is so strong and flowing all over the place that they appear overtly as tense, anxious people. In a sentence, such people can be described as those who always have to find something to worry about. For this reason they make very bad group leaders because they make the group feel tense and not very safe.

The fourth type is one whose basic belief is that all the love and good things are out there in other people. Therefore they say, 'I need to so manipulate all those other people so that I can get my fair share'. This is called the hysterical type person. They often make the statement 'I simply love people' and claim to find other people 'interesting'. They do have a potential to be a group leader because they are energised by a genuine love of people simply because they need them for their own wellbeing. The snag is that such people give up easily in adversity and get so emotionally involved in the group that they cannot see the wood for the trees. In the short term, and where all is well, such people really make a group tick, but over a longer period their manipulative activities tend to start a counter reaction which leads to the demise of the group.

The fifth and final type lacks what the hysteric has, and has what the hysteric lacks. It is the schizoid personality. They are overtly cool, self sufficient people whose intellect is strong. Their agenda is, 'Other people's emotions can trap and hurt, so distance yourself, play it cool and do not trust them. Rely on your own judgements'. Frank Lake points out that in many people the hysteric and the schizoid lie close together and the cornered hysteric can become schizoid, just as the cornered schizoid can become hysteric. The strength of the schizoid is the ability to become detached from the emotional situation and reflect intellectually on what is going on. The weakness is that they can switch off and distance themselves so much that they get out of touch with the group. Bearing this weakness in mind as a real limitation such people can make good group leaders.

In conclusion, it is obvious that no one of these personality types on their own makes a person a good leader because they only describe emotional responses to certain threatening situations. Having, however said this, one can claim that the best equipped is a person with the right balance of schizoid and hysteric, together with just a touch of overt anxiety that will make them aware of the feelings going around in the group.

We now turn to a method of personality assessment that does not start from the negative, but attempts to describe people just as they are. Many prefer this approach because they feel that it is non-judgmental and therefore more freeing. It is known as the Myers Briggs personality type indicator and has a Jungian basis; a useful book on it is *Knowing Me Knowing You* (Malcolm Goldsmith and Martin Wharton, S.P.C.K.). This book is worth reading because it explains the system well and also has the means for self-assessment in it. As with Clinical Theology, it is better to go on a residential course for an accurate assessment, and the typings are fluid in that they can change with the emotional and spiritual growth of the individual.

Myers Briggs gives sixteen types with much more subtle variation than those of Clinical Theology. They are built up by assessing the balance of certain attributes of the personality. Eight attributes are assessed and balanced against each other in four sets of two. All eight are present in everyone but four of the eight are usually stronger and it is those ones that give the personality type. Change takes place when the 'shadow' or weaker factors grow in strength and eventually gain more balance with the stronger ones. The eight attributes are:

Introvert	(I)	or	Extrovert	(E)
Intuition	(N)	or	Sensing	(S)
Thinking	(T)	or	Feeling	(F)
Judging	(J)	or	Perceiving	(P)

Whichever of the two opposites is the stronger is assessed by a series of questions relating to a person's response to certain situations. A simple definition of each is as follows: The introvert (I) draws energy from within, therefore when tired has to withdraw from others, while the extrovert (E) draws energy from others, and therefore needs them around for strength and encouragement. The intuitive person (N) thinks by use of insights and awareness, suddenly has flashes of inspiration and works out the implications afterwards. The sensing person (S) has to have all the evidence and lots of data before they can work out answers – rather more slowly than Ns, but they tend to get things right more often.

The thinker (T) does not trust emotions and often cannot sense what others feel. This person can be a ruthless businessman who gets things done, whereas the feeling person (F) is always concerned about what others will feel, and therefore tends to get bogged down. Such people are bad at business but good artists and tend to be governed by their emotions. Judging (J) and perceiving (P) are not so easily defined. In general it can be said that a (J) person is only happy when everything is cut and dried, whereas a (P) person prefers not to make definite decisions until all possible information on a subject has been assembled. Often they fail to make decisions because they are not able to collect enough information to satisfy themselves. As opposed to this a (J) person moves on by making decisions, at times without knowing enough facts, getting it wrong and then making another decision to correct it.

This method of assessing describes people as ENTJ, ISFP, ESTJ etc, ending with sixteen types. As far as group leadership is concerned no one type will conclusively make a good leader because it depends on the degree to which specific attributes are present. For example, if a person is 18 points F and only 2 points T, they will be able to sense what is going on in a group, but will become so bogged down by it that they cannot lead, whereas one who is 11 points F but 9 points T will do quite well. On the type indicator both would register F. A 19 point T person would be hopeless at leading a group because nothing would be picked up emotionally but 11 points T and 9 points F would do well.

Extroverts and introverts (E and I) have the same problem as (T) and (F). The same applies to (P) and (J). Intuitive thinkers (N) tend to be born group leaders, but because they are instinctively on the ball in a relaxed way their clear sense of strategy can make them block out the group's creativity.

In conclusion, it would seem that on the basis of this personality assessment, the people most likely to be good group leaders are those whose opposing attributes are fairly evenly balanced, except for N and S Intuition/Sensing where a higher level of N is desirable.

Charles Handy's assessment of leadership styles is more from a sociological standpoint than a psychological one. In his book, *Gods of Management* (Pan Books) he categorises styles of management based on four of the gods of ancient Greece, Zeus, Apollo, Athene and Dionysus. These gods of the old pagans, as St Augustine points out in *City of God, book IV* have no reality in themselves but are projections of human beings. Professor Handy uses them in this way as mirrors that reflect back to us an image of what we are like.

The first, Zeus, is symbolized by a spider in the middle of a web. Zeus was the king of the gods and was supposed to be able to have the other gods on strings to pull in when he wanted. He was the centre of the network and was manipulative, controlling people like a spider in a web. If we are a Zeus type character, when we lead a group, our style of leadership will really be getting everybody on a string, keeping it tight and controlled, so that nothing can happen unless we allow it. This is a very limiting style for a group leader because it limits the whole group to the talents of the leader. A degree of manipulative ability is essential, but it must be used carefully. Where the leader is a weak or frightened person, manipulative skills can destroy a group because they will always be used for the leader's own security and not for the group's benefit. The group will eventually sense this, rebel, and the unity of the group is destroyed. This style of leadership is also very exhausting for the leader and creative of negative tension.

The next type of leader is modelled on Apollo. This leader works by using a rigid system. There are a lot of Apollo leaders in the Civil Service and in Armies, where everything is graded. Ranks in the German Army are called 'Ober', everyone is over someone, no one is 'Unter'. That is typically Apollonian because its distinguishing feature is that everyone is conscious of status and rank. The Apollo type of leader will tend to look at a group and pigeon hole everyone in it. There will be knowledgeable ones and less knowledgeable ones, ignorant ones and very ignorant ones. All will be categorized, some will not be allowed to say too much, while others will, according to where they have been put in the status list.

The Apollo type is symbolised by a very beautiful symmetrical building with all the nice windows in the right place and everything neatly in order, pens and pencils assembled correctly and neatly arranged in a very rigid type of structure. It is easy to see that such a style of leadership is not relevant to the needs of a small group. It would suit a paranoid person, who, as we have already seen, does not associate with small groups.

The third one is the Athene type. It has a criss-cross network as a symbol, because Athene is a sensitive task-orientated type of person who likes to know what everyone is feeling and where everyone stands all the time. Such a person is always taking the temperature of the group and aims at keeping everyone happy. The Athene leader feels that a good group is where everyone is happy and will go to any length possible to ensure this. Athene leaders would run happy but inefficient businesses.

As group leaders, such people would fail by not allowing problems in individuals to come out in the open, or negative tensions to develop because they could not handle them. Their inner agenda would register these as failure and they would resist them so strongly that the work of the group would be blocked. There is a high level of anxiety in such people which is unconsciously transmitted to the group, making the insecure members feel unsafe. However, they are often very good assistant leaders because of their sensitivity.

Finally, the Dionysus type. This type is very intuitive, sharp and astute, can see small things clearly, but cannot cope with big things.

They are the kind of person who is very aware of what is going on in one person at a particular time, but cannot relate to a large number of people at once. An interesting thing about these Dionysus types is that they all do their own thing and are all a bit eccentric. Therefore they will rise to a special occasion and are brilliant in a crisis but they cannot actually just plod along. The Dionysus type leader would never run an industry but is very prevalent in the caring professions, especially among people like doctors, clergy and solicitors, where they may deal with a few people at an intense level. These characters make good group leaders and counsellors but may be carried away by their own enthusiasm. In Clinical Theology the Dionysus type is of the schizoid type with some hysteric, in Myers Briggs he or she is high on intuition.

Another sociologically based method of assessing leadership styles is that of P F Rudge. In his book *Ministry and Management* (Tavistock, London) he describes styles of leadership as follows:

1. Traditional   2. Charismatic   3. Classical
4. Human relations   5. Systemic

The traditional leader believes that his or her role is keeping a tradition going. Their thinking is, 'We have handed to us a tradition, we have always done it this way, this is the right way to do it, therefore I as leader am here to see that the tradition is kept and no one is allowed to challenge it.' What matters most is that everybody is made to toe the official line at all times.

The strength of this style of leadership is that it does keep things stable, but a traditional style of leadership only applies to secondary groups because secondary groups are by their nature stabilising. Thus a primary group with this type of leadership cannot function as a primary group and it will be destroyed.

Rudge's second type of leadership style is described as charismatic, not in the theological but in the sociological sense, meaning a person whose character is of rather a flamboyant nature. This type of person is parallel to a Dionysus type in many ways, but not entirely. They have individual flare and draw certain people to them, like a magnet, where one end draws and the other repels. Many adore them, waiting upon their every word, but others absolutely hate them. This type of leader prevails in small group leadership. They do have problems in that their groups consist of people who are setting them up on a pedestal. Such groups will not do any real work in opening up because the charismatic leader often blocks other people from challenging them. When challenged, the charismatic leader tends to act in a judgmental way that will reject them and push them out. This is the weakness of a charismatic leader. They are less able than Handy's Dionysus type at holding a group together. They are often found leading small groups that are self appointed in that they are just people coming together drawn by the magnet. These groups grow and collapse very quickly.

Rudge's third type is the Classical. Classical leadership is very hierarchical, roughly equivalent to Handy's Apollo. The classical leader works by putting everyone in their right pigeon holes of importance. Like the traditional type, this leadership style is more applicable to a secondary or tertiary group, but in a primary group, people will just be trapped in their pigeon holes. Any movement or growth will be killed off because some people's comments will be accepted and others rejected or treated as of less value depending on their place in the leader's hierarchy.

The fourth type of group leader, rather like Athene, Rudge calls 'Human relations'. Human relations leaders are dedicated to keeping everybody happy. This means that such leaders get worn out very quickly because they expend so much energy just in not allowing anything unsavoury or which might rock the boat to come up in the group. This style of leadership will work well for a while until the leader gives up with exhaustion. It is such a vulnerable style of leadership that in the end the group destroys it. There are often in any group or organisation a few manipulative people who latch on to the human relations type of leader and really tear them apart. This makes them very depressed, sad and low. Often they cannot see why this happens and say such things as 'I am so tired, I do not know what it is, but somehow or other life is becoming such a struggle and I only want to put it right'.

It is the inner agenda to be good, kind and get it right that is this person's weakness. They need to be needed and cannot risk failure, and so are very vulnerable to themselves and others. They can however, lead some groups well if supported by someone with experience and understanding.

The final type is the Systemic. This one is a bit on its own, but relates a little to Apollo and Zeus. The systemic is a rather crafty sort of person who tends to sum up what is going on in the group, then evolve a system by which they manage the group. These people are often very successful, because they do tend to develop considerable expertise. They have quite a flair for handling people, but their weakness is that sometimes the group will rebel against them, because they will feel manipulated, especially if there is a strong personality present who has made a bid for leadership. The systemic person will sense this and try to outwit them. This tends to result in all sorts of battles not all of which are creative. Their main object is to have a system that works, and they are quite willing to adapt anything to the group to achieve this. For this last reason alone, systemics make good group leaders, but as with all things human they do have their blind spots.

These five methods for assessing personality with a view to discovering one's suitability for group leadership are guidelines only to stimulate self understanding. They are means, not ends. They do help people to be more realistic about their own strengths and weaknesses. Therefore they are valuable for spiritual growth and development of the individual even though they show that few people are the right type to be good leaders of small groups.

The majority, therefore who come to the conclusion that small group leadership is not for them, will have gained not lost by acquiring this self knowledge, because whatever they end up doing in the service of the kingdom of God will be more realistic and therefore more likely to be in accordance with God's will. Clement of Alexandria, a second century Church Father, said, 'The greatest of all lessons is to know oneself: for if someone knows himself, he will know God, he will become like God'. It is in knowing ourselves truly that we get to the point of knowing our need of grace. Self knowledge alone is not knowing God but a positive step on the way. Leading small groups is but one aspect of the whole of ministry. If it is yours, get on with it, if not leave it to others. The following passage of scripture states this quite plainly.

> Now there are varieties of gifts, but the same Spirit; and there are varieties of service, but the same Lord; and there are varieties of working, but it is the same God who inspires them all in every one. To each is given the manifestation of the Spirit for the common good. To one is given through the Spirit the utterance of wisdom, and to another the utterance of knowledge according to the same Spirit, to another faith by the same Spirit, to another gifts of healing by the one Spirit, to another the working of miracles, to another prophecy, to another the ability to distinguish between spirits, to another various kinds of tongues, to another the interpretation of tongues. All these are inspired by the same Spirit, who apportions to each one individually as he wills.
>
> (1 Corinthians Chapter 12, verses 4-11).

Chapter X

The Leader's Spiritual Life and Wellbeing

After reading the previous chapter on personality types and styles of leadership, one could justifiably feel like saying, 'There is no point in reading on because it is impossible that I could lead a group. I am not the right type!' This, in God's eyes, is only true up to a point. He seems to choose all sorts, Jeremiah, for instance (Jeremiah, Chapter 1) who in other ways are most unsuitable. This would mean that if you happen to end up leading a group, and your personality is such that you are not a natural group leader, the stress on you will be greater, or you may appear very incompetent and have a group that is not 'run by the book'. However, you may well by the grace of God enable much of benefit to happen. This points to the reality of 'Vocation'; God chooses whom he wills for purposes known only to himself. This is his sovereign right and at times it will appear to cut across all accepted human principles. Besides this it is also possible that a person could enable much of benefit to happen in a group without actually being a leader. Aware and spiritually alive group members are very great enablers. Therefore do not go away and say, 'I am useless because I am not in "this" or "that" category'. You might well be a good number two in a group and the dynamics of a group are such that the leader needs assistance, support and feed-back. When I lead a growth group, I always like a woman who is a 'human relations' type with me to pick up what is going on in the group and feed it back to me, because I often miss it due to my own personality type, even though it should make me a good group leader!

The simple fact is that we are all limited, even by the gifts and strengths we have been given naturally by God. We cannot be one thing without not being another. We forget this, and in our society this tends to put some people on pedestals, but the theological approach enables us to

147

see that in the body of Christ, every member has a function. The last chapter showed us that it is important to come to terms with, and be honest about, what we are really like so that we have some idea about how God is most likely to use us and what our function is within the body of Christ – the church – in the local area. It is not about writing some people off.

Having said that, no matter what we do in the way of pastoral work, whether it be counselling, leading a group or general pastoral care, there is going to be a general wear and tear upon us; we are going to get worn out. It is a fact of life that people wear us out, get us down, drive us up the wall, make us angry, and have all sorts of effects on us when we try to love and help them. Although we can have pain without love, we cannot have love without pain. It is learning to cope with the pain of loving and caring that I want to deal with in this chapter.

I see this primarily as a spiritual thing. If we have a total dependence on ourselves and take a humanist stance that man is the measure of all things, this will make us try to be self-sufficient and omnicompetent. Then we cannot cope with anything of other people's pain at any depth, and will have to cut ourselves off from situations and block out things that hurt us in order to survive. This in turn will force us to rationalize by saying either that 'these people are this or that', thereby writing them off, or we will have to find some bag of psychological tricks to pull out to deal with them. The end result will be that we demean the humanity of either ourselves or other people in order to survive. If we are to cope in a Christian way and follow Our Lord, a bit of the cross with its agony and suffering is going to come in and we are going to get hurt. I want therefore to spell out one or two rules and insights about coping with the hurts that come from the wear and tear of pastoral care in its various forms including group leadership.

A very basic insight with regard to coping with the hurts, stresses and strains of pastoral care is the Dynamic Cycle, a diagram of which is given below.

The Dynamic Cycle

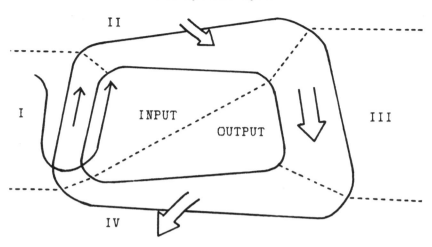

Phase I	ACCEPTANCE	makes 'being-itself' possible
Phase II	SUSTENANCE	feeds and sustains being
Phase III	STATUS	motivation, out-going movement
Phase IV	ACHIEVEMENT	of service for others

This, as illustrated, was devised by Dr Frank Lake, founder of the Clinical Theology Association. What it says, in simple terms is – that you cannot give out without taking in. As human beings, if we give out, give out, give out . . . we empty ourselves: so we have to take in to replenish the energies lost.

Leading a group and caring for people is a continual 'give out'. It is true that we can do these things in order to boost our own ego (ie take in), but if we do, we will not help others very much. If we are giving out – that is our 'achievement' (on the Dynamic Cycle). We can only achieve anything if we have the grace to do it. Jesus said, 'Apart from me, you can do nothing' (John's Gospel, Chapter 15, verse 5). What he meant, was that we have to have input, and the input part of our lives is based on us feeling that we are accepted and loved by God just as we are, whether we are 'human relations' type, systematic, traditional etc . . .

If we do not believe that we are loved and accepted just as we are, we will become a pretty tense person who feels the need to prove ourself by striving to achieve recognition and earn love. This will feed back to every group we attempt to lead and block off the process of growth and healing within it. Experiencing and living with an awareness of ourselves as a person who is lovable and acceptable is the basis of a kind of praying that will help us to be relaxed enough to lead a group. This will be looked at in more detail later.

The second phase in the dynamic cycle to acceptance is sustenance. We need to be sustained and strengthened in our experience of love and acceptance. This sustenance needs to come from both our prayer life and other people. It is important to have a soulmate with whom we can share our deeper thoughts and feelings, including our hurts, in an atmosphere of love and acceptance. Our relationship needs to be so secure that they can also challenge us, question what we say and really make us think. It must be an honest relationship as well as a loving one and it needs to have a good degree of commitment from both sides.

Our input phase, just described, is taking in both spiritual and emotional strength, which I believe, go together. An interesting book called *As Bread that is Broken*, (P van Breeman S J, Dimension Books) would help with this. It is a book of meditation and prayers on getting this dynamic cycle right, so that we have input to enable the necessary output. If we have the right input, then we are given an identity, status and a selfhood. A person who has good status can say, 'This is what I am like, and I am happy to accept what I am like. Anyway, God will love me and use me in whatever sphere I can operate as a person'.

When we are able to act in this way, it can be said firstly that we have not only got the dynamic cycle of our lives working properly, but also that we have a real relationship with God that enables us to see beyond the immediate situation of our present agonies. There is, as Alcoholics Anonymous believes, a power outside and above us on which we need to rely, and this reliance is not just a matter of words.

Secondly, we need to have an affirming relationship with one or two other people. Together, these two facts give us the strength to be aware of our own inner weaknesses, our fears, despair etc, and not to be overwhelmed by them. They also give us the strength to be 'crucified' by others who may need to put on us their own agonies as part of their own process of healing. This 'being crucified with Christ' is something we need to recognise, accept and live through. Only when we have grace to do this we will be able to operate as a group leader with any degree of efficiency.

Thirdly, all these things together in practice is a fulfilling of the great commandment to love God and our neighbour as ourselves (Matthew's Gospel, Chapter 22, verses 37 and 39). This is because it gives the autonomy from which to be truly loving in a committed, determined and real way. Autonomy can be described as being a real person, before God and in relationship to others. This is essential. The following old tale illustrates what happens when this autonomy is not strong enough.

The miller went to market with his son and his donkey – the miller and his son leading it. When they went through the first village, the village gossips in the square said, 'Look at those two silly people, they have a donkey and neither of them rides on it.' The miller heard this, so when they got out of the village he said to his son, 'You sit on the donkey.' So the son sat on the donkey. When they went through the next village, the gossips said, 'Look at that disgraceful thing. There is the old man walking and the young man riding the donkey.' So the old man said, 'I will sit on the donkey,' and the boy led the donkey. At the next village, the gossips said, 'Look at that. There is the young man walking and the old man riding the donkey – that is disgraceful.' So they got out of the village and scratched their heads, and the miller said, 'I know what we will do, we will both ride it.' So when they got to the next village, the gossips said, 'Look at that. Cruelty to donkeys.' When they got out of the village they did not know what to do, so they both got off the donkey and carried it. Now as they were going into the town over the bridge, the town folk ran out and said, 'Look at those two silly fools. They have a donkey and they are carrying it,' and they started jeering at them. At that, the donkey took fright, jumped in the river and was drowned.

This story illustrates graphically what happens to a group whose leader does not have enough autonomy. He or she is so influenced by what is said in the group that it ends in chaos because the leader crumbles under the stress and strain placed on them by its members. Lack of autonomy leads to an inability to be firm, make decisions and carry them out. As opposed to the negative illustration in the story, we get a more positive example from St Paul. Many people react strongly against him and always have done, but this is a sign of good leadership, and all good leaders will share his experience. This is what he says in his first letter to the Corinthians (which is applicable to anyone involved in spiritual leadership in any form).

> People must think of us as Christ's servants, stewards entrusted with the mysteries of God. What is expected of stewards is that each one be found worthy of his trust; not that it makes the slightest difference to me whether you, or indeed any human tribunal find me guilty or not; I will not even pass judgement on myself. True, my conscience does not reproach me at all; but that does not prove that I am acquitted; the Lord alone is my judge, there must be no passing of premature judgement.
>
> (1 Corinthians Chapter 4, verses 1-5).

What Paul was saying here was that he had enough autonomy, so that what he was doing was what he believed God had called him to do. Therefore he was going to get on and do it. This basic belief made him able to take a certain amount of stick, tension and criticism. I believe that this sort of autonomy is totally conditional on whether we have the right relationship with God. Only if our prayer life and our relationship with God is right can we have that sort of autonomy. It does not mean that we should not listen to people or accept what they say; but that we should listen, then think and pray about it, and finally make our own mind up. Being democratic is another thing entirely. This is, for example, where the human relations leader is weak because they try to keep the peace and be democratic. A democratic approach is out of the question in small group leadership because it does not expose inner truth or stimulate spiritual and emotional growth.

One very important issue in our relationship with God must be mentioned. Jesus said, 'Not everyone who calls me Lord, Lord, shall enter the kingdom of heaven' (Matthew's Gospel Chapter 7 verse 21). Another saying that illustrates this point is 'You might know the language of Sion but it does not make you a member'. Our lives must in reality be based on a trust and love of God that comes from truly knowing him or else we will find ourselves uttering empty words. We may in theory be right, but others will sense that within we are empty. Our prayer life must be one that gets us in touch with God and at the same time makes us aware of what is going on in our own inner life, if we are to have the emotional and spiritual strength to cope.

One way of helping with this is to keep a journal. Ira Progof has developed a method of journal keeping. He shows how there is what he calls 'a river within', whose resources we can tap by his method of writing a journal of our own lives, whereby our pen becomes a 'tool of the unconscious'. (At a journal workshop, Dialogue house library, NY, 1975). This is the same as that which some mystics experience and it is the mystical, contemplative approach to prayer which is necessary for the development of our inner spiritual resources. Some prayer exercises which you may find useful are outlined fully in Chapter II, and you may also find some guidelines on contemplative prayer helpful here.

Contemplative prayer is really a mystery which is far beyond the grasp of the human intellect and can never be fully explained. However, it can be experienced and partly understood. It is about making spiritual contact with God that is beyond words and or thought. Saying prayers uses words and meditation uses the mind, but contemplative prayer starts with us being totally passive and allowing God to come to us and show himself to us spiritually.

Contemplative prayer requires two things, regular commitment and perseverance over a long period of time, and this involves a lifestyle in which this commitment is a high priority. Silence is also essential, together with a special place in which to sit or kneel. Many people use a special prayer stool but no one particular posture needs to be taken, just one in which one is at ease so that the body is not physically stressed. Some people like to sit in front of a candle, icon, simple cross or crucifix, but many just like to get into a comfortable posture and close their eyes.

The principle behind such prayer is firstly the sovereignty and priority of God. He created everything. He initiated redemption through sending Jesus into the world, and he will conclude all things when he considers the time is right. Therefore, an act of contemplative prayer is passive on our part. It is waiting on God and opening ourselves up to him so that he can act as and when he wills. Secondly, it is the belief that God loves us and we can trust him fully, whatever we might experience. This trust is very important to enable us to enter the stillness of soul that is required.

What can I expect to happen? At first some agony and pain will be experienced as all those unresolved emotional hurts within begin to surface. Some people relive past traumas with great intensity. When this stage is worked through, then a time of peace and inner quiet comes. This is the beginning of a stage known as the prayer of quietness and most people can expect to reach this. The next stage is a feeling of awe, emptiness and a great awareness of things spiritual giving a new dimension to our understanding of the world. Then can come a time of ecstasy when one feels oneself outside the world. In this stage one cannot easily bring oneself 'back to earth' but must wait for it to happen. Finally, some people can have a vision of the uncreated light, and a very few, a sense of unity with the Godhead.

There are dangers to this kind of praying. We may become confused and get 'out of our depth', or in the early stages become defeated by the pain and struggles involved and misinterpret what is being experienced. Therefore, a wise and experienced guide who can give support and help us to understand what we are experiencing is essential. The bottom line is wanting it badly enough to stick at it.

Chapter XI

Some Helpful Guidelines and Techniques for Group

Leaders

The aim of this chapter is to give some basic guidelines for those engaged in leading a group. The object of this is to help the leader to be both in touch with what is going on in the group in terms of individual's agendas and to be effective at enabling the work of the group to be carried out. These two objectives are the basic functions of the leader from which everything else follows.

The first point is that the leader should make the group members feel safe and relaxed. Most people are anxious and a little tense anyway. This is inevitable, but as the group get to know each other and its group identity forms, a safe relaxed atmosphere should develop. The key to this lies in the personality of the leader. However, there are a number of small practical things that can be done which are little in themselves but all contribute to creating a place of safety.

Seating must be comfortable, of equal height, and arranged in a circle so that people face each other. If there is a table in the centre for any reason, it must be low, so that eye contact is possible for everyone. Lighting is important; it must be low, warm and gentle. If possible an open fire is a good focal point and the room temperature should not be too hot or too cold. Anything else that creates a warm homely relaxed atmosphere is of value, but it must not be overdone. In a less than ideal setting the personality of the leader can overcome other deficiencies, but if the leader is not relaxed and confidence inspiring, then these other factors, even when ideal, will not help very much.

The second important point is that the leader should control the group in such a way that there is freedom for honest expression and encouragement for contributions from all members to be offered. Control is important because where this is lacking, strong bids for leadership take place and the weaker members get pushed down. On the other hand, over control is also destructive leading to frustration that explodes in bursts of destructive anger rather than creative energy. In short, the leader should be in the role of firm referee whose function is to apply the rules only where necessary and in such a way that the game goes on in a naturally flowing manner.

These are the rules that will help to ensure this:

(i)   Involve every member at every meeting. To do this, the leader must concentrate on all that is being said, both verbally and in body language. Those who do not say anything should be invited to do so but not pressed. Examples of how to do this are:
a) Look straight at the silent member or members and say, 'Mary/ George, you have not spoken yet. Is there anything you would like to say?' Sometimes there is, but often not. What matters most is that everyone gets a chance to speak and it is the leader's responsibility to enable this to happen.
b) Note the body language of members who say little, and comment on it as a way of letting them in. Look directly at them and say for example, 'Ann, your foot is going up and down, I wonder what it means. Is it trying to say something?'

(ii)   If what has been said is carried out properly, then group dominance by one member, or power struggles, are less likely to develop. If they do, it is better for the whole group to confront the offending person or persons. For this, the leader needs to say something like this to the group: 'Fred has now spent ten minutes asserting his views. I would like to ask each member of the group to make a response to what he is saying'. This approach often opens up something very creative and strengthens the leader's positive control. Some may see it as manipulative but the ability to manipulate wisely and in a creative way is an essential part of group leadership. Those who cannot do this will lose control and respect. It must be remembered that the group is an organism in itself, not individuals fighting one another. It is within this very basic concept that the legitimate manipulative functions of the leader must be understood.

The leader is there to allow the energies of individuals to work and interact in a way that holds the group together in creative tension and provides a structure within which individual members can receive grace. Two passages from Paul's letters illustrate this; the first one from his first letter to Timothy on the characteristics of a leader (Greek EPISKOPOS = one who has oversight, sometimes translated as 'Bishop').

If anyone aspires to the office of leader, he desires a noble task. Now a leader must be above reproach, married only once, temperate, sensible, dignified, hospitable, an apt teacher, no drunkard, not violent but gentle, not quarrelsome, and no lover of money. He must manage his own household well, keeping his children submissive and respectful in every way, for if a man does not know how to manage his own household, how can he care for God's church? He must not be a recent convert, or he may be puffed up with conceit and fall into the condemnation of the devil, moreover he must be thought well of by outsiders, or he may fall into the reproach and snare of the devil. (1 Timothy Chapter 3 verses 1-7)

The second from Paul's letter to the Ephesians:

And his gifts were that some should be apostles, some prophets, some evangelists, some pastors and teachers, for the equipment of the saints for the work of ministry, for building up the body of Christ, until we all attain to the unity of the faith and of the knowledge of the Son of God, to mature manhood, to the measure of the stature of the fullness of Christ; so that we may no longer be children, tossed to and fro and carried about by every kind of doctrine, by the cunning of men, by their craftiness in deceitful wiles. Rather, speaking the truth in love, we are to grow up in every way into him who is the head, into Christ, from whom the whole body, joined and knit together by every joint with which it is supplied, when each part is working properly makes bodily growth and upbuilds itself in love. (Ephesians Chapter 4, verses 11-16)

(iii)   Thirdly, prayer, and its correct place in a group is a very important issue. Prayer that is misplaced and inappropriate is destructive, and in some ways is not prayer at all. For this reason, many people in groups ignore prayer, being afraid of its dangers, but sadly missing out on its positive side. Several important principles apply if prayer is to be of value. The main one is that the leader should sense the flow of energy in the group and be aware when it is leading towards prayer. Part of Paul's letter to the Romans is relevant here:

> Likewise the Spirit helps us in our weakness, for we do not know how to pray as we ought, but the Spirit himself intercedes for us with sighs too deep for words. And he who searches the hearts of men knows what is in the mind of the Spirit, because the Spirit intercedes for the saints according to the will of God. (Romans Chapter 8, verses 26-27).

A person who is in tune with the group, and also prayerful themselves will be led to pray at certain times, either verbally, or in silence. This usually happens at the end of a group, or at some point when the group is working well, but rarely, if ever, at the beginning. The danger with opening with prayer, or forcing prayer on a group is that it can act as a block to its work and be a defence against facing real issues. This is why it can be claimed that inappropriate prayer is not prayer at all.

(iv)   Point four can be summed up by two words, Confidentiality and Respect. The leader must firmly insist on these two things and spell them out from time to time.

Confidentiality means that everything said in the group and all that happens in it is the group's property and must not be taken outside the group or gossiped about. This rule, if firmly kept, gives security and freedom to members so that they are able to work out very sensitive individual agendas within the group. Respect means that everything said by individual group members is handled in a non-judgmental way. People must be encouraged by the leader to work out the implications of statements they make for themselves, by questions that draw them out and not by dogmatic corrections. The leader must also be firm in not allowing other members to give dogmatic answers and thereby crush exploration. When a leader does this well, others in the group pick up the message and the whole ethos of the group becomes one of respect. This results, as time goes by, in the problem of respect being a non-issue. In love it becomes a habit as the group knits together in a supportive, but at the same time, creative and challenging way, giving the members an experience of what Paul's letter to the Ephesians mentioned earlier means in practice.

The final point is that the leader must draw out and use the experiences and expertise of the whole group. It is important to remember that it is more important for the leader to ask questions than give answers. On some occasions, the leader should give an answer, but only when asked a direct question. If all direct questions are avoided, the leader will lose authenticity in the eyes of the group and this in turn will put a block on the group's creative work.

The other aspect of this point is allowing other members of the group to take over the leadership when they have something special to offer the group. The leader who can do this without fear of losing control is one who is confident about their leadership ability and has established good rapport and respect within the group.

We will now look at two modern therapies that offer techniques to allow leaders to apply the guidelines mentioned above. They are Gestalt Therapy and Transactional Analysis.

Gestalt Therapy is German in origin and was begun by Fritz Perls in the 1930s in America. His theories were first put into practice as the 'Human Potential Movement' (*Gestalt Therapy Now*, eds. J Fagan and I L Shepherd, Penguin, 1972, and *Gestalt Therapy*, Perls Heppertine and Goodman, Dell Publishing Co.). A more recent book of value is *Gestalt Counselling in Action* by P. Clarkson, Sage Publications, reprinted 1994. Gestalt Therapy is also called the third force because in its approach to psychological problems it lies somewhere in between Analysis and Behaviourism.

Gestalt is a German word with no exact English equivalent. In practical terms it means making a pattern whole or complete. The aim of Gestalt

Therapy is to bring this about within a person by increasing their self-awareness, completing unfinished things within, such as a desire to do or be something, which is blocked by fears or other negative emotions, and to do this in a way that is acceptable and relevant to life as lived in the present.

This therapeutic approach applies to group leadership because there are three Gestalt rules which when applied to a group situation bring hidden agendas out into the open, in such a way that the group's energies can be directed towards helping the individual come to terms with painful issues in a creative way. The three rules are:

i) Here and Now   ii) I and Thou   iii) Not Why?, but How?

i)   Here and Now – This rule makes people face up to issues in the present, especially painful ones. There is an avoidance of this in all of us which leads to fanciful theorising, trips of nostalgia, complicated explanations and clever side stepping. A good example of this can be seen in John's Gospel (Chapter 4 verse 7), where Our Lord is in conversation with the woman at the well of Sychar. When he was about to pin her down to discussing her real problems she deflected him by bringing in a secondary issue concerning the temple on Mount Gerazim (Deuteronomy Chapter 11, verse 29). She did this with a style that can trap many, being very flattering, but Our Lord cleverly took it up and used it in a positive way. 'Sir', she said, 'I see that you are a prophet. Our fathers worshipped on this mountain, while you say that Jerusalem is the place where one ought to worship'. Jesus did not enter into the discussion she was trying to set up, but came back at her about her own spiritual state in a direct way. 'You worship what you do not know,' he said, and then went on to comment, 'God is a spirit, and those who worship him must worship in spirit and in truth.' Another example of Our Lord dealing with people in this way can be seen in Luke's Gospel, Chapter 5, verses 21-25 and Mark's Gospel Chapter 8 verses 27-30.

The group leader must always deal with what group members say by a direct approach, and not be led astray by 'red herring' issues. If this is not done, others in the group will follow the red herring and annoy those who want to get on with the real business. The 'Here' part when applied, means in the present context of life as it is being lived by every member of the group. How other people live outside the group is not relevant. The 'Now' part is at this moment, not how group members felt or behaved last week or at any other time, but how they feel at this every minute. The Here and Now rule when wisely applied keeps both the unity of the group and the individual agenda of the group in a creative balance that energises the whole group. It prevents disintegration and stagnation.

ii)   I and Thou – This rule is aimed at making people responsible for themselves. It makes people talk *to* each other and not *about* each other and thereby avoids gossiping that is negative. It also helps individuals to grow into responsible adults capable of managing their own lives in a responsible way. Our Lord applied this to the apostles in St Matthew's Gospel when he was talking about the issue of Messiahship. Beginning with 'Who do people say the Son of Man is?' he finally focuses on 'Who do you say I am?' (Matthew Chapter 16 verse 13). In a group, the leader must focus issues in a similar way. He or she does this by taking issue with any member who says, for example, 'St Augustine said this', or 'the bishop says that', or 'one believes this', by saying, 'But what do you feel about this issue?' and if relevant, coming in by saying, 'I feel this or that . . . what do you feel?' In short, this rule takes all issues out of the third person, impersonal and general, into the first person particular. By so doing it helps group members to relate to each other in a very human way.

iii)   Not Why? but How? – This rule involves people becoming aware of the emotional content of what they say. Why? is a very intellectual approach to a problem and enables the emotional content to be removed or covered up. How do you feel about this or that issue elicits an emotional response. As individual agendas are highly emotionally charged, the question 'How do you feel about this?' brings out into the open something that could tick away under the surface like a time bomb and explode at a difficult time, possibly in such a way as to destroy trust in the group. Asking, 'How do you feel?' at an appropriate time, for example when body language shows some agitation going on under the surface, or when someone is off on a long explanation of why such a situation exists, can prevent a group from drifting into a negative situation.

There is, of course, more to Gestalt Therapy than these three rules, but the insights demonstrated here will put a valuable tool into the hand of any group leader. We will now look briefly in a similar manner at the value of insights from Transactional Analysis for group leadership.

Eric Berne, the originator of Transactional Analysis, based his approach on the theory that in each adult person there are three centres of awareness, or 'ego states'. These are Parent, Adult, and Child. When two people interact in any relationship, one of these ego states tends to predominate, which will be different at different times and in different relationships. The value of this to group leaders is that it gives a useful map of interactions which can be used to understand why certain people in the group relate to the leader and others the way that they do. For more information than can be given here, two books worth reading are *Transactional Analysis in Psychotherapy* (Eric Berne, NY Grove Press 1966) and *Games People Play* (Eric Berne, Penguin).

For the practical purpose of equipping the average group leader for the task in hand, all that needs to be recognised is what each ego state is, how it expresses itself in an interaction, and what action needs to be taken for the work of the group to continue in a creative way.

i)   The Parent ego state records and stores in the central nervous system events perceived by and impressed upon a person mainly by the adult world, as their personality develops during childhood. Parents, teachers and other emotionally significant people feed into the developing child concepts of right and wrong, good and bad, thereby creating patterns of acceptable behaviour. The activities of conscience are also developed giving the individual an internalized moral code. When an adult person is speaking or acting from the parent ego state, they tend to be dogmatic, judgmental and prejudiced or protective, defensive and apparently self-assured in their behaviour.

ii)   The Adult ego state is the mature adult part of an individual which is able to transform stimuli from the real world of the here and now into data that can be processed, filed away, and brought to bear with relevance on any new situation which may arise. As it is that part which finds things out for itself, one of its tasks is to modify the Parent state by bringing it up to date as it experiences new situations. It also examines the feelings of the Child state, carefully sifting them and only acting upon them if they are relevant or valid.

iii)   The Child ego state is created by the recording of internal emotional responses in babyhood and early childhood based upon how the whole environment was seen, heard, felt and understood at that period of the person's life. These recorded feelings are both negative and positive. Harsh, unloving and misunderstanding social conditioning by the adult world at this stage of development can leave a person with such a damaged ego state that in adult life they continue to respond in the manner of a hurt child, whenever similar situations to those which caused the hurt in the first place are experienced. Conversely, the person who had a happy childhood will continue to exhibit in adulthood childlike delight, curiosity, discovering urges and creativity when the relevant situations prevail.

Bearing these ego states in mind, two important factors must always be taken into account. Firstly, all three ego states are present all the time in every person. Secondly, through the variety of interactions possible within every group, situations are bound to be created that strike a chord in the parent or child of one or another group member. Because of this, a whole variety of responses will take place that do not relate to the here and now business of the group. We will now look at how these can be understood and dealt with using this Transactional Analysis (TA) approach as a tool.

Firstly the leader must be able to recognise what is happening. In his or her mind must be a clear concept of what a child or parent response is like, together with a sensitivity of approach to point this out. For example, a situation could arise in which a person becomes very angry every time another person contributes something. The leader notes that this is happening, and observes carefully the nature of the transaction. If the angry response always takes place when dogmatic, judgmental statements are made, then it can be assumed that the angry response is child to parent. When the leader has observed this, then it is pointed out to those involved and an invitation to explore what is happening is given. This then provides valuable material for the whole group to work on, giving each member a chance to become aware of his or her own parent or child behaviour.

It is also valuable for a group to have a session on understanding the basic principles of Transactional Analysis early on in the life of the group. This enables them all to participate more fully in the group's activity and helps to prevent a situation from developing in which the members of the group operate from their child and the leader from the parent position. If this happens all creative possibilities are crushed. There are of course a very wide variety of interactions possible between people within a group. It therefore takes time and experience to be able to recognise them. The one cited above is a very simple and basic one. In order to provide a wider basis of understanding, a few examples of different types of interaction, called by Eric Berne 'Transactions' (hence the name 'Transactional Analysis'), are given below. These should provide a would-be group leader with enough information to be able to recognise the most likely types of Transactions that take place, and especially the difference between a Complementary and a Crossed Transaction.

COMPLEMENTARY TRANSACTION – one which is appropriate and expected. It tends to get a predicted or predictable response, following the 'natural order' of human relationships.

———→ This represents the statement the first Person makes.
← – – – – – This represents the response to the statement.

P	P	Sick man, little boy like: 'I don't feel well.'
A	A	Caring wife, kind mummy 'You have a rest and I
C	C	will get you a drink.'

P	P	'We ought to':
A	A	'Yes, we ought to at once'.
C	C	

P	P	'What news?'	P = Parent
A	A	'I got the job'.	A = Adult
C	C		C = Child

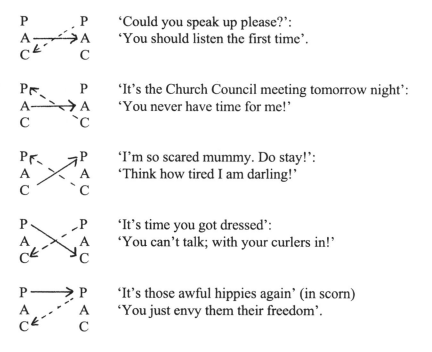

P   P   'Let's have fun!'
A   A   'Quick, in here'.
C ⇄ C   Excited, daring

All these are healthy in a relationship and serve to strengthen it, because they are appropriate.

CROSSED TRANSACTION – one in which the stimulus statement 'hooks' an inappropriate response, which is often hurt/hurtful, disappointed/ing or unexpected. These tend to be conversation stoppers or lead to mutual recriminations.

P   P   'Could you speak up please?':
A ⟶ A   'You should listen the first time'.
C   C

P   P   'It's the Church Council meeting tomorrow night':
A ⟶ A   'You never have time for me!'
C   C

P   P   'I'm so scared mummy. Do stay!':
A   A   'Think how tired I am darling!'
C   C

P   P   'It's time you got dressed':
A   A   'You can't talk; with your curlers in!'
C   C

P ⟶ P   'It's those awful hippies again' (in scorn)
A   A   'You just envy them their freedom'.
C   C

These are unhealthy because they undermine a relationship by being inappropriate and not in the 'here and now'.

A golden rule for getting business done efficiently in a group is that the leader should endeavour to keep all the interactions/transactions in the adult to adult ego states. This is the only way anything can be discussed rationally. This involves skill, maturity and some genuine manipulative ability on the part of the leader. Good chairmen of committees have this skill, usually combined with a natural authority given only to people with real leadership skills.

Finally, the leader of a small group must help all the members to see what they are doing so that the leader is not just playing a kind of Transactional Analysis god game with the group. As already mentioned, it is a good principle that all members of the group be taught to use the Transactional Analysis tool so that they can use it on themselves and each other. Sometimes this can be done little by little as the group develops, but in some groups a session can be devoted to teaching the basic principles. As with all group work, the leader has to be able to sense where the Holy Spirit is leading and respond accordingly. A good leader who is in touch with God can mediate the grace of God by use of wise manipulation with a group that is working well.

Chapter XII

Groups for Spiritual Growth

This is such an important issue that one chapter will be entirely devoted to looking at it. Human spiritual development cannot take place in isolation from other human beings. Spirituality cannot be taught by purely intellectual didactic methods because a sound spirituality must involve the whole person and it is to do with relationships; with God, the spiritual world and other human beings. The intellect does have a place in spiritual growth and learning, but a secondary one, that of reflecting upon and giving meaning to experience. The experience must come first to provide the data for the mind to work on, otherwise a twisted and unsound spirituality will develop.

An adequate illustration of this point can be shown by an examination of love. The basis of the Christian Gospel is that 'God so loved the world that he gave his only begotten Son'. This is an intellectual statement made by the use of words, but what does it mean? It is easy to make such statements but not so easy to live them out in our daily lives. Love is the key word, and no amount of explaining or theorising can get its meaning across to a person. It has to be experienced by the whole person, especially by their emotions, to be understood fully. The nature of love is that it can only be experienced in a relationship with another person or persons, and at least one person has to love us unconditionally before we can become open to further explorations in love.

Human love, important as it is, is limited and of different varieties. I would like to include a journal extract here as an example:

At prayer this morning, I was seeking grace to love those who are broken and empty and need unconditional love. I interceded for several whom I know. As I did this, it came to me that God is love and therefore to experience real love is to experience God. I was flooded with a powerful love, the same as that I have experienced from those who really love me, but much more powerful. I saw God's love as an unlimited ocean from which human beings can take it only by the bucketful; no more, because it becomes too heavy to carry. When our bucket is empty, we need to fill it. If we do so from another human being's bucket, we empty it and they then can love no more. I prayed that I may never fill my bucket, which is so often empty, from the bucket of those who love me, but from God, so that I can share what is in my bucket with them and let the contents of our buckets mix and mingle. That is the nature of human loving and God's love.

Two books worth reading are *The Art of Loving* (Eric Fromm, Unwin pop Psychology reprint 1987), and *The Four Loves* (C S Lewis, Fount Paperback, Collins). The Christian belief is that God is Love, and is the originator of all love and loving. Therefore Christian Spirituality must have its roots in a love and loving that is ultimately rooted in God. People grow and are stimulated spiritually when they are exposed in key relationships to this love of God, and are given the support to discover both its negative and positive aspects. A group for spiritual growth is the milieu for this to take place, and a basic model is that of our Lord and the twelve apostles which could be called the first Christian primary group.

A group for spiritual growth must therefore be a group in which love is experienced, explored, reflected upon and made meaningful to individuals. This involves a high degree of negative emotion which can be frightening and painful. It also contains mystery, paradox, and at times, uncertainty, but underlying it all must be a commitment to truth, personal integrity and an enduring patience. All this was expounded by the prophet Hosea:

> When Israel was a child, I loved him,
> and out of Egypt I called my son.
> The more I called them,

the more they went from me;
they kept sacrificing to the Baals,
and burning incense to idols.

Yet it was I who taught Ephraim to walk,
I took them up in my arms;
but they did not know that I healed them
I led them with cords of compassion,
with bands of love,
and I became to them as one
who eases the yoke on their jaws,
and I bent down to them and fed them.

They shall return to the land of Egypt, and Assyria shall be their king,
because they have refused to return to me.
The sword shall rage against their cities,
consume the bars of their gates,
and devour them in their fortresses.
My people are bent on turning away from me;
so they are appointed to the yoke,
and none shall remove it.

How can I give you up O Ephraim!
How can I hand you over, O Israel!
How can I make you like Admah!
How can I treat you like Zeboiim!
My heart recoils within me,
my compassion grows warm and tender.

I will not execute my fierce anger,
I will not again destroy Ephraim;
for I am God and not man,
the Holy One in your midst,
and I will not come to destroy.

(Hosea Chapter 11 verses 1-9)

This passage shows both the negative and positive aspects of love, but above all it shows that its initiative must come from the lover toward the loved (in this case, God towards mankind), and if it is real, it will not dry up, but will persist and work through the negatives until it overcomes them. This is what a Christian ministry must offer. If this ministry is by means of a primary group, it needs to have within the group all the New Testament fruits of the Spirit, as outlined by Paul in his letter to the Galatians, which will need to find their focus in the leader: 'But the fruit of the Spirit is love, joy, peace, patience, kindness, goodness, faithfulness, gentleness, self-control' (Galatians Chapter 5, verse 22).

For this reason a group for spiritual growth must as a priority be led by a person of emotional stability and mature spirituality, whose faith has been tested and who is able to love and be loved without strings attached. This would argue for someone of at least middle age who can provide a sense of security in which the insecure and fragile of faith can feel free to express themselves honestly, without condemnation and superficial corrections. The leader must be much further along the road than other members of the group, but not without doubts at times. Age alone does not bring this, but without the necessary years it cannot be achieved to the degree required.

It follows that when love, both human and divine is actively experienced in a group by means of the relationships within it, spiritual growth within that group becomes a possibility. It is the discovery of the inner truth that an individual needs to know in order that the growth might take place. This is in fact the purpose of the group but it cannot be attempted until the right relationships are established so that love in its supportive aspect is being experienced. Human beings can only look into the dark recesses of their souls when there is the correct external support to provide the security for this to be undertaken. When this is established in a group and the inner search begins, only then can the painful side of love be accepted and experienced in a positive growth creating manner. Because people who want growth and tend to go for growth groups lock, stock and barrel, also tend to want to get into the work of plumbing the depths quickly, there is always a danger that this aim will be frustrated because time will not be given for the right supportive relationships to develop and love to be experienced enough in the early stages of the group. This will greatly harm the more sensitive persons and put many outside the scope of benefiting from group work. The leader, therefore, must be strong in control for the sake of giving everyone the freedom to explore at their own pace. The twin rules of respect and confidentiality are the means of this control and should be firmly enforced by the leader. A leader who is intuitive enough to sense the movement of the energies of the group and the movement of the Holy Spirit will be the only one able to lead successfully in this area.

'Truth in the inward parts' or 'inward being' (Psalm 51, verse 6) is the first objective of a group for spiritual and emotional growth. In order that a person should grow in spiritual strength and become complete (perfect) as Our Lord commands (Matthew's Gospel Chapter 5, verse 48) many deep things within need to be exposed, so that they can be understood and dealt with in the appropriate way. This is a very difficult process because these truths in the inward parts are not understood by the intellect alone, nor are they verifiable by it. They are truths about our very being and nature itself, as Jesus Christ implies in his command to be complete as God is complete; they involve truths outside the individual as well. These are truths about God, his creation, and his purpose for us as the highest form of that creation, with power to create and destroy. When we consider them, we are into the realm of mystery. We are dealing with something that will always be too big for us as human beings to handle, but at the same time so present and real that we must come to terms with it to the best of our ability.

This fact causes many to shy away and stick with what is controllable by human effort alone. This can be called the common sense approach of wisdom and humility, but in the scriptures, God seems to be calling his people on to launch out into the deep, take risks, and by so doing, discover his richness, power and glory. What is more, he promises to assist those 'foolish' people who are willing to do this by sending them the Holy Spirit. Jesus promises this to all who desire to know God, grow in faith and eventually become the people God created them to be (John's Gospel, Chapter 16).

Spiritual growth, then, starts with a need to know 'truth in the inward parts', but it does not end there in a situation of holy navel gazing. It leads those properly engaged into a more realistic and enriched relationship with God, other people and the world. It also leads towards growth with no defined limits in this world but to a consummation in eternity. In understanding how a group can help people to discover their own truth in the inward parts, it is important to look in a little more detail at what the scriptures are saying.

The first problem with this is that of our intellect. We must make intellect our servant and not our master. We must be secure enough in well being to either engage or ignore our servant intellect, but never despise it. In our modern world we tend to make intellect our master, serve it slavishly and without question until it makes us its own dehumanised slaves. Many, having become slaves of intellect, become totally incapable of facing the truths necessary for spiritual and emotional growth, because their intellect rules out the validity of anything other than itself. As a result the message of the scriptures is not received as God offers it to us and the work of the Holy Spirit is either blocked or misunderstood. On the other hand, some react against the intellect and despise it altogether. This leads to emotions running riot and smothering spiritual growth.

It is important to get a right balance in a group for spiritual growth between emotion and intellect. This can only come about through competent leadership and an understanding that allows the Holy Spirit his place.

Now let us look in more detail at the biblical principle of 'Truth in the inward parts', the basis for understanding the work of a group for spiritual growth. Inward parts means hidden or covered things. There is a great deal in scripture about God and his purposes being hidden because people would not be able to cope with it. Moses could not look at God and had to cover his face (Exodus Chapter 3 verses 4-6). In the New Testament, St Paul says that God reveals the hidden things of the human heart (1 Corinthians Chapter 4 verse 5), and even the purposes of God are hidden until the right time for them to be revealed (Ephesians Chapter 1, verses 3-10, and Chapter 3, verses 7-20).

In Psalm 50, verse 6, the Hebrew word Tuchoth seems to come from the root of a word meaning to overlay or to cover, so it literally means 'the covered things'. The word appears elsewhere only in the book of Job, when it refers to hidden signs written in nature (Job, Chapter 38 verse 36) but its use there may be dependent on our psalm passage, hence any translations are almost guess work. Two explanations are open to us.

i) The 'covered things' could refer to the physical human body. They could be heart, kidneys, veins, etc. – the inward parts.

ii) The 'covered things' refer to things unseen, that is to say they are 'obscurities or mysteries'. Even though modern translations seem to favour this, perhaps because of its point of contact with modern psychology, there is no certain way of strictly deciding which is meant by the author. However, for our purposes it is sufficient to say that human beings do have many covered up things that need to be exposed for their own health's sake, and that this is the purpose of our groups for growth as it is in psychoanalysis.

The Hebrew word Emeth (truth) is used very widely in the Old Testament. It can also be translated faithfulness and has the sense of something sound and reliable. Truth in Hebrew is not intellectual, but carries the idea of 'Foundation', something solid on which to build. It includes intellect, but also with it the emotions on an equal footing, that could be described as a sense of wellbeing. We need in life, a sense of trust, and to get this we need to find the bedrock of our existence; this is God who is mysterious in his whole creation including man. Each person has within their soul a dark inner continent, which throws up all sorts of threatening powers that need to be grappled with and overcome. This dark inner continent is related to wider hidden things that cannot be discovered by intellect alone. (mysteries and and Job's obscure signs). Intellect must be used to reflect upon and understand these things we discover in the hidden places. We are afraid of them by virtue of the fact that we are human. Therefore three important factors in this discovering of truth are:

(i) The risen Christ must come with us into the dark places of the soul to keep us safe.

(ii) Other people must hold our hand (metaphorically speaking) as we make the discoveries.

(iii) The Holy Spirit must direct.

A group for spiritual growth is a practical way of carrying out this work so directly and simply described in the words 'The truth shall make you free'. (John's Gospel Chapter 8, verse 32). The freedom given by Jesus Christ is a freedom from fear and domination by negative forces that dehumanise us and make us incapable of relating to others in love. These powers that come from both within and without, but mostly from within, can only be freed and overcome when a sound foundation is present from which to deal with them. In the first place the love and respect of those in a group begins to supply a foundation. From this a growing faith in, and awareness of the presence of the Risen Christ completes the foundation of trust from which the terrors of the inner dark continent can be exposed and freed (Psalm 91, verses 5-6).

A group that is set within the context of prayer and the Eucharist provides the second deeper foundation, and it is an interesting point that in a follow up of those who undertook primal therapy sessions with Frank Lake in Nottingham towards the end of his life, those with an awareness of the presence of Christ were able to get deeper into their pain and receive more healing than those without this (Dr Roger Moss' research into primal therapy at Lingdale, Clinical Theology Association).

Having set out the principles on which a group for spiritual growth is based, let us conclude on a practical note by giving three 'ways in' to the discovery of inner truth.

The first one is simple and most effective, therefore should be widely used. It is for the leader to invite the group to relax, breathe deeply, and allow whatever is in them to come to the surface. This includes feelings, images, deep experiences, in fact, almost anything. After about five or ten minutes of this, the leader invites individuals to share with the group what they have experienced. There are two ways of doing this, and neither way should be followed all the time. The first way is to say 'Who would like to share first?' then wait for someone to start. The other is to invite individuals by going round the group in a systematic way. If the first method is chosen, the leader must ensure that everyone has a chance to share their experience by the time the session ends. The other important point to remember in this method is that group members should be told that they are free to make a response to any other group member, or experience another person shares, in an honest direct way. This method allows all sorts of responses to be made that lead to awareness of inner truth because members spark off each other's individual agenda. The leader is important in enabling this to happen. In the silences, he or she should pray for the enlightenment of the Holy Spirit so that they can stay with what is happening spiritually as well as emotionally and be enabled to pray openly only when the time is right.

It is obvious that for this method to work the spirituality and emotional maturity of the leader is vital and the best way to learn this method of leadership is to spend a period of apprenticeship in a group with a leader of experience. Just reading up on the method does not equip a person to do it.

The second valuable technique is the use of pictures. The leader at the onset should explain that one does not have to be an artist and any form of symbol is always acceptable. This approach always gets in touch with someone's negative social conditioning and elicits responses like 'Oh no, I cannot draw. At school they always told me it was not worth my bothering with art'. This of itself is a way in for a competent group leader, who could respond with something like 'Well, just present a blank sheet of paper and we will explore what you feel about it'.

One use of pictures is to invite the group to draw a picture of their relationship with God as it now stands. The method for doing this is:

i) Give each member a blank sheet of paper and have available in the centre of the group a box of many different coloured felt pens.

ii) Tell the group to sit silently for five minutes thinking about what they are going to do.

iii) Next tell them they have ten minutes to draw.

iv) When the drawing time is up, divide the group into pairs. Then tell one person in each couple to put their picture in front of their partner and let their partner tell them what they see in the picture. The person whose picture is being examined must remain silent.

v) After four minutes, the person who drew the picture can tell their partner what they intended to portray and enter into a discussion about anything that comes out of either the differences or similarities relating to the drawer's intentions and the partner's observations.

vi)   The process of 'iv' and 'v' is then repeated allowing the other partner to present his or her pictures.

vii)   Finally the whole group shares, comments and responds to each other's experiences with the leader ensuring that everyone has a chance to contribute.

The third useful help is the use of fantasy journeys. This is a valuable tool for exploring the 'inward parts'. Since it is worthwhile also to consider the purpose and spiritual dimension of fantasy journeys we will spend longer on it, and so it will be the subject of the next chapter.

Chapter XIII

Fantasy Journeys for Spiritual and Emotional Growth

What is a fantasy journey? A fantasy journey is an exercise in which people are led by using their imagination, into hypothetical situations that enable them to explore their own inner fantasy world. *A Dictionary of Pastoral Care* defines 'fantasy world' as follows: 'The whole imaginative life of the mind, conscious or unconscious, which underlines and structures all thinking and all action'.

As this definition indicates, people are not like blank sheets of paper upon which the experiences of life write a story. From conception we are complex and delicately balanced organisms which respond to the stimuli that come from our environment in a variety of ways. It is out of this particular interaction that each one of us builds up our own particular fantasy world, which becomes the means by which we interpret the world in which we live and also the behaviour of other people in relation to ourselves. These fantasies, therefore, affect us morally, intellectually and emotionally by setting up within our minds many images of good/ bad, right/wrong, beautiful/ugly, desirable/undesirable people and situations. They are the active basis of all our prejudices and value judgements. For this reason they are very important and should be taken seriously.

A good early childhood nurture will give us a positive inner fantasy world that helps us relate well with our environment and interpret it with a high degree of accuracy. A bad early childhood nurture will give us a negative one, by which we will often misinterpret the world outside and the behaviour of others towards us. People who have had a bad nurture will often inflict their bad fantasies on us because by so doing they will reduce their own inner pain. Any person in a counselling, pastoral, or any other form of helping role will experience this.

177

The process of personal growth also involves people putting parts of themselves, in fantasy terms, into others, and taking parts of others into themselves. For growth we all need good experiences and encouragement to work out our fantasies so that we can be helped to build a positive fantasy world within, which in turn will help us to have good relationships with the world and other people. We also need them to give meaning to our lives, to help us make decisions, and come to terms with everything we experience. Understanding the nature of our fantasy world and knowing how to help it become healthy is an important part of counselling and pastoral care, and guided fantasy journeys are a useful tool in helping us to explore and understand this inner world.

Guided fantasies help us to develop as whole people by re-activating our neglected fantasy world. Many people block off or deny their fantasy world. For example, day-dreaming is an important part of our fantasy activity but so often as children we are told not to day-dream and the result of this is that many people feel guilty when they do. The imagination, that is, the ability to understand ourselves and our relationships with others by use of pictures rather than words or abstract ideas is then crushed and our fantasy world repressed, denied or distorted. This denial and blocking off also inhibits our ability to perceive some truths of a spiritual nature that cannot be understood by purely rational means.

Guided fantasies help us come to terms with negative attitudes. Since many people's lives can be blighted by negative fantasies which adversely affect their ability to make sound decisions and relate well to others, guided fantasies can help us by exposing these negative things so that we can come to terms with them and develop healthy self-awareness. From this point people can experience a freedom from some compulsive behaviour patterns and prejudices, thereby enabling them to make more realistic decisions about changing their attitudes and responses to others.

Guided fantasies help us to know ourselves better. We all tend to live our lives on the surface and so often struggle against strong emotional undercurrents that make living more of an uphill struggle than necessary. Guided fantasies expose these undercurrents. Sometimes this comes as a shock when first experienced because we are aware for the first time that we are not the person we thought we were. There are also times when we find things that encourage us, but in both cases a healthy amount of self-knowledge is always beneficial in the long run.

Fantasy journeys also have a spiritual dimension. They can be of use in our prayer life, since by opening to our conscious mind aspects of ourselves that could have remained hidden, they can help us relate to God in a more meaningful way. Thus we are enabled to open ourselves up towards God in a deeper way and allow to his Spirit to search us out – essential for spiritual growth. (Psalm 139, especially verses 23-24).

Guided fantasies are also of benefit in understanding scripture. The rationalistic approach of Biblical scholarship in modern times has had the negative effect of causing many to miss the point that the scriptures are trying to make. An analogy from art should make this point clearer. Anyone standing in front of a great painting can feed the soul from its beauty, absorb what the artist is trying to say and respond to it with one's whole being. This is a very humanising and uplifting process. The rationalistic approach does not have this wholesomeness. In analyzing from a scientific basis it just reduces the picture to certain quantities of chemicals, no different from all other chemicals. This approach does nothing for the soul of man, it just leaves it barren, dull and empty.

God speaks to man through the scriptures in a very deep and mystical way which is hard to define accurately. The Holy Spirit is active in this communication and we as individuals need to respond with our whole being, not just part of it, and in an honest way. Prejudices and fears that come from our fantasy world can distort this response. Guided fantasy journeys can help us recognise these distortions so that we can seek the grace of God to rectify them and allow God to speak to us more accurately through the scriptures.

Ignatius Loyola used this approach in his spiritual exercises, their value being their use of the imagination as an aid to devotions based on the scriptures. For example in his exercise for meditations on the 'Kingdom of Christ', where one is invited to consider how Jesus was born, Ignatius says:

Form a mental image . . . See the persons; Our Lady, St Joseph, the servant girl and the child Jesus after His birth. **Become** a poor, miserable and unworthy slave looking upon them and ministering to their needs **as though present there. I will then reflect within myself** in order that I may desire some fruit. (*Spiritual Exercises of St Ignatius*, p71, Image Books.)

This quotation shows how Ignatius used the guided fantasy method as a means of helping the individual to enter the spirit of scripture, thus enabling them to comprehend its message in a full and meaningful way. The important practical aspects of using fantasy in the study of scripture are highlighted. They can be summed up in five words:

Imagine   **See**   **Become**   **Be Present**

In practice we are helped to get in touch with the eternal qualities of the Gospel by this approach.

We now come to consider the practice of guided fantasy. Although it can be done individually, it is best done in groups of eight to twelve and is therefore ideally suited for work with small groups.

Leading a group

Begin by telling the group to relax by sitting or lying in any position that is comfortable for them and to close their eyes. When they are in this chosen position ask them to breathe deeply, slowly, feeling the air entering and leaving their nostrils. Secondly, lead them through the three zones of awareness.

Zone 1   External sounds such as clocks ticking, wind, traffic, birds, singing, others in the room. Ask them to select the sounds they can hear one at a time. Listen attentively for a while, then tune them out.

Zone 2   Feelings of discomfort caused by not being in an entirely comfortable position physically. Invite people to have a final shuffle until at ease.

Zone 3   Existing thoughts not left behind, such as memories from work eg 'Did I switch the computer off? I must tell the boss that in the morning', or from home, 'I wonder if the babysitter is OK? It was nice seeing X this afternoon, I wonder if he felt the same about me!' Invite people to collect up their thoughts and leave them behind in preparation for a new journey.

When this is all completed start the journey you have chosen in the manner described from the Ignation exercises . . . ie imagine you are . . . see, hear, smell the surroundings etc . . .

At the end of the journey invite the members of the group to return to the here and now by opening their eyes, looking around the group and making eye contact with them. Ask them to take their time, and do not move on to the next stage of sharing experiences of the journey until everyone has made this eye contact.

Each person in the group then shares what they experienced during the fantasy, and all members should feel free to respond to other people's experiences and make comments. This sharing is very valuable, but dogmatic interpretations of other's experiences should be avoided. The aim of sharing is to help individuals explore and interpret their *own* experience and the leader must be firm about this, as well as the issues of confidentiality and respect within the group for everything shared.

There are several important points to remember about the sharing of experiences.

i) Some people who are tense, or so full of pain that they cannot let their inner fantasy world flow freely, will block off and not get into any aspect of the journey. This must be accepted because in time as they feel safe within the group they will be able to take part.

ii) When those just described above begin to relax after several experiences of fantasy journeys, they usually get partial ones, which must be explored, accepted and respected because they will in time lead on to fuller experiences.

iii) As each fantasy journey deals with where a person is at the time it is done, whatever they experience should never be seen as saying something permanent about them. Everyone has a fantasy world which runs on its own and cannot be manipulated, only blocked off. This world within us reflects accurately where we are in spiritual and emotional terms at any one time. To get in touch with it is to make contact with a valid part of our real selves.

iv) It is a good idea to note down our fantasy journeys for future reference and also make them material for our prayers. This aids spiritual development.

v) Sometimes through guided fantasies we open up within ourselves past hurts that can be frightening. For this reason people must not be forced to share in a group more than they feel able to cope with. It is also wise for people who experience 'bad' things in fantasy journeys to seek counselling and spiritual direction from an experienced person in this sphere.

vi) Blocking off can manifest itself in the following ways: going to sleep; saying 'I don't have an imagination'; 'This is all stupid, I live in the real world' etc etc. Group leaders should be patient with them because once they feel safe enough to let go, their fantasy world will come into its own and surprise them. They will usually say something like, 'I was amazed at the images going through my mind, things I would never have thought of and I had no control over them, they just happened'. This sort of statement indicates how frightening and enlightening our fantasy world can be.

Which fantasy journey should I use? This chapter closes with two examples of fantasy journeys, one taken from an account of a healing miracle in Luke's Gospel (Luke, Chapter 5, verses 17-26) and the other is one suitable for a growth group as a means of exploring how we relate to others and they to us. A book by John O Stevens (*Awareness: Exploring, Experimenting, Experiencing*, available from Eden Grove Ed. 26, Eden Grove, London N7 8EF) contains many, but it is advisable for those who wish to lead fantasy journeys to experience them first by being in a group led by someone experienced in this sphere, until they have a good awareness of their *own* fantasy world. From this point some good journeys will be learnt off by heart, others can be made up, especially those based on the Gospel stories.

The main skills required are to get the right speed, pause in the right place, having a sensitivity towards others and a relaxed confidence about it all. A good apprenticeship with a balanced and experienced person who is wise in pastoral care and not just 'reading it all up', is the only way to achieve this.

Fantasy

The Healing of the Paralytic (Luke Chapter 5, Verses 17-26)

You are lying paralysed and helpless in your room when some friends burst in to tell you that they have heard of this man Jesus who heals people . . . he is just down the road and they want to take you to him. What are your feelings? . . . is it an easy choice for you to go to Jesus? . . . who are the four friends who will carry you? . . . take time to choose them carefully.

Now they carry you along the road . . . what is it like? Imagine the dusty road . . . as you near the house you are aware of a great crowd . . . your friends put you down and investigate . . . how do you feel now? . . . They rush back and say they are going to let you down through the roof . . . what are your thoughts and feelings as they do this? . . . slowly, slowly, they lower you through the roof, you can see their faces peering down . . . now you are level with the people's heads . . . what do you sense now? especially as some of them are hostile to Jesus . . . a sudden silence and you are at Jesus's feet . . . how does the crowd react? . . . how do you feel?

Jesus stands beside you and says quietly 'Your sins are forgiven', he looks round at the crowd, then takes you by the hand saying 'Take up your bed and walk' . . . what is this moment like? . . . to be face to face with Jesus? . . . to be upright again and walking? . . . what do you do next? . . . now walk slowly away from that place . . . in your own time return to this room and to the group.

Some things to ponder:　attitudes to healing
　　　　　　　　　　　choice of friends
　　　　　　　　　　　dependency/independence
　　　　　　　　　　　trust
　　　　　　　　　　　forgiveness
　　　　　　　　　　　faith

Projection fantasy

Get yourself into a relaxed position, close your eyes . . . become aware of your breathing . . . the steady rhythm of air going in and out . . . in and out . . . notice any sounds inside the room or out, tune them in then tune them out . . . now pay attention to your body . . . is there any pain or discomfort, tense each part of it then relax it . . . have a final shuffle to be really comfortable . . .

I want you to think of a person alive now to whom you really relate and admire . . . work out what it is that creates the rapport . . . take some time to do this . . . now I want you to imagine that they are coming into the room where you are sitting . . . what are your *feelings* as they approach?

Repeat this paragraph saying . . . a person you dislike intensely etc

then . . . a person who likes you and looks up to you

then . . . someone who gets at you and dislikes *you*

. . . now I want you to leave your four people and come back slowly into this room . . . indicating you are back by opening your eyes and looking round at the group . . .

This can now be debriefed in small groups or twos to discover what people think and feel is going on in these relationships . . . where the positive and negative feelings really belong . . . to me? . . . to them? . . . to some other significant person in life? . . . discover if there is some mirroring or projection going on.

Chapter XIV

Groups for Support and Supervision

THE ETHOS OF THE GROUP

This section closes with a chapter containing some general thoughts on groups for support and supervision. I begin with a quotation by St Augustine of Hippo. St Augustine wrote in the late fourth and early fifth centuries when the Roman Empire was in a state of collapse. His main theme is that in this world we have no lasting city, civilisation or indeed anything from which we can get values or principles that will last and give us security. We must therefore seek to find them within an eternal city with eternal values based upon the Kingdom of God focused in the words of Jesus, 'Heaven and earth will pass away, but my words will never pass away'.

In our time the same kind of collapse is taking place for the same reasons as the Roman Empire collapsed. In such conditions there are always increasing numbers of hurt and crushed people. We who seek to help them from a Christian standpoint must beware that we are not crushed and brought down with them. Neither must we be fooled by the remedies and smooth talk of this collapsing world which cannot face its own collapse because it has nothing else. We must look to our faith, to the wisdom and discernment that God the Holy Spirit gives us in Christ, and from that starting point build up our own groups and support systems. I will now let St Augustine speak:

> To help us form our judgement, let us refuse to be fooled by empty bombast, to let the edge of our critical faculties be blunted by high sounding words like 'peoples', 'realms', 'provinces'. Let us set before our mind's eye two men; for the individual man is like a single letter in a statement, an element, as it were out of which a

185

community or realm is built up, however vast its territorial possessions. Let us imagine one of the two to be poor, or poorer, in a middle station of life, while the other is excessively rich. But the rich man is tortured by fears, worn out with sadness, burnt up with ambition, never knowing serenity of repose, always panting and sweating in his struggles with opponents. It may be true he enormously swells his patrimony, but at the cost of those discontents, while by this increase he heaps up a load of further anxiety and bitterness. The other man, the ordinary citizen, is content with his strictly limited resources. He is loved by family and friends, he enjoys the blessings of peace with his relations, neighbours and friends; he is loyal, compassionate and kind, healthy in body and temperate in character, and enjoys the serenity of a good conscience. I do not think that anyone would be fool enough to hesitate about what he would prefer. (*City of God*, Book IV, Chapter 3.)

There are three issues raised in this passage by St Augustine that are relevant to the spiritual dimension of groups which counsellors or pastoral carers may support or supervise.

(I) The contrast between the 'Rich' (in this world's understanding) and the 'Poor' or 'Ordinary Person'.

The stresses and tensions experienced by those whose ambitions are of a worldly nature are largely self-inflicted by the values of such people. The more successful they become, according to their own terms and values, the worse and deeper their problems become. Such people are ultimately self-defeating for three reasons.

(i) What they strive for can never be fully achieved. The law of diminishing returns makes this impossible. The harder they strive for inner satisfaction, the less satisfied and more inwardly restless they become.

(ii) They use what energies and gifts they have mainly to achieve status in the eyes of other people. They can never therefore totally relax and become ordinary natural human beings in the presence of others for fear of losing this status, and with it their own identity. The result is that they become tense, afraid, isolated and unable to communicate in any meaningful way. In short they make themselves 'sub-human'.

(iii) Their values, and the criteria by which they judge others and themselves is imposed in a cruel and harsh manner. This makes them the victims of a very demanding lifestyle which deprives them of the resources and energies required to live it out with integrity. They thereby make themselves slaves of a tyrannical master and in turn become tyrants themselves, the outcome of which is destruction.

The 'Poor' or 'Ordinary' person represents those whose values are of the Kingdom of God. These people base their lives on the values set out in the gospels, on the teaching of Jesus Christ. Worldly success is not of great importance to them, and should it come as a by-product of their lives, it is just accepted as something that happens on this life's pilgrimage. Life is seen in terms of a pilgrimage in which many things are experienced, some good some bad. Worldly success and failure are both the same, just experiences which can, if dealt with wisely, enrich our journey towards eternity. Indeed, many would say that experience of both is essential for our full development as people. Psalm 49 expresses this well, punctuating the message with the following words repeated twice, in verse 12 and at the end:

'A rich man without understanding; is like the beasts that perish'.

Those truly living by the principles of the Kingdom of God will appreciate this point because for them life is a series of varied experiences, good, bad and indifferent, all of equal value because all can be the stimulus that helps one grow in grace. Only the truly wise understand this.

There are three points of importance concerning those living the Kingdom of God.

(i) Such people achieve without always being aware of it because they are not primarily concerned with personal achievement but with doing a good job for the sake of it, or even for the love of it. This attitude leaves much openness to the grace of God. I Corinthians, Chapters 1-3 express this, and especially Chapter 3 verse 6: 'I did the planting, Apollos did the watering, but God made things grow'.

(ii) The support such people need comes, in human terms, because they value the cultivation of loving creative relationships with people whom they respect and to whom they have a commitment. Within such relationships it is possible to laugh, cry, be angry and express all kinds of emotion, both positive and negative, without fear of rejection, of being despised, manipulated or used in a power struggle for selfish advantage. (iii) The values by which they judge themselves and others come from within their own self-awareness and their own inner experience of the workings of God in a human life. It is not imposed by a harsh and demanding master, one who does not give help or encouragement. This is because the starting point for all who live within the rule of God's Kingdom originates in the unfathomable, inexhaustible love of God as mediated through Jesus Christ. St John's Gospel Chapter 1, verses 1-14, tells us this, ending with the final statement:

> The word was made flesh,
> He lived among us and we saw His Glory
> the Glory that is His as the only son of the Father,
> Full of GRACE and TRUTH. (JB).

(II) Empty Bombast

Augustine uses this term for words that sound good, but when carefully examined, either have no meaning at all or cover up something sinister, whose outcome is the opposite to that which seems to be implied. Politicians in all the power structures of the world do this, it is a part of their trade or craft. It happens to be the way things are because of the flawed nature of mankind.

Such things creep into the church at all levels simply because it is part of this world and includes all the faults of this world on which Satan can get to work. Hence Our Lord's parable of the tares sown in the wheat (Matthew Chapter 13 verses 24-30). The world of counselling and pastoral care is not exempt from this and has its own politics. This cannot be avoided, but we must be aware of it, examine carefully those elements of 'empty bombast' that are potentially present, and not let them deceive or master us. Let us now look at a few of the key words used in this field and test them for their potential to become 'empty bombast'.

The basic meaning of the word, 'supervision' is to oversee someone else, to cast an expert eye over them, to make sure that their work is up to standard and to see that the system being operated is functioning properly. In itself this is perfectly straightforward, but it is when we look at the emotional aspects of being a supervisor, or supervised, that dangers begin to appear.

Let us now look at the range of feelings possible for a person who is engaged in supervising. They could, for example, fear losing control of the situation and become too rigid or demanding. This would make them tense and they could as a result perform less well and miss something vital. Some people could develop a feeling of superiority that could lead to a sense of infallibility, the sense that they are always right and the supervised always wrong. People with a variety of emotional inadequacies, but a sharp intellect or other gift of above average measure, could well use the position of supervisor as a means of boosting their own ego by manipulating the supervised and using them to prove to themselves that they are OK. Others could well feel that supervision is just another way of earning money, something boring that has to be done because we all need money to live. Such people would not have the motivation to probe into difficult areas, and so not be very competent, even though they may on paper be highly 'qualified'. Finally there are others who could feel that being a supervisor is a vocation, a sacred task given by God that is not an easy one, but must be entered into with diligence. Such people would be very prayerful and careful knowing that the well-being of others depended on them.

In our terms, only the last reason is acceptable as a basis for supervising, but because we live in an imperfect world, any or all of the others may be present. The important thing is that they must be recognised and dealt with honestly. Failure to do this can cause the word supervision to become 'empty bombast'. It is our lack of inner awareness and true spiritual life that renders us all liable to make any word into this.

Those who will suffer most and be dealt an unfair deal when supervision is allowed to become 'empty bombast', will always be the supervised, and eventually their clients.

The point that I am most concerned to make is that it is largely due to the way that our emotions work behind the words used and the purely intellectual meaning they have that creates the problem St Augustine calls 'empty bombast'. Therefore it is very important that these emotions be recognised, understood, accepted and dealt with in a realistic way. The most realistic way I know is one that has a good balance of the emotional and spiritual, together with an appropriate use of the intellect. I believe that this aim is best achieved in the context of a sound, well led group and not by individual one to one supervision. There is, I consider, a place for some one to one supervision, but only as a back up to a group and for specific problems and situations. More will be said about this later, but for the moment I would like to offer a few more words that have the potential to become 'empty bombast' and say just enough about them to stimulate your own reflections.

(i) Professional – This could convey, on the positive side, meanings of discipline, competence, obedience to a strict ethical code and trustworthiness. On the other hand in the experience of some it could be a cover up for incompetence and inner weakness, one big act of deceit, a means of gaining status and a breeding ground for paranoia.

(ii) Accountability – The question this raises is to whom? This defines its meaning. Are we accountable to good or evil, God or the devil? If our accountability is limited to a small area such as the organization we work for, the client, the government or any group or individual, being accountable to them could mean that we are in a position to be manipulated by them for their own ends.

(iii) Authority – This is essential for any group or organization to function properly and someone must exercise it. This must, however, be the right person with the right qualities or else it can become a corrupt, empty and destructive thing. So many incompetent and evil people have used this word in a destructive way because they have done so in order to cover up their own fears and inadequacies.

(iv) Support – This could mean encouragement to grow strong and cope with life, but also simply a negative prop creating an unhealthy dependency.

I would suggest that these words, and perhaps a few others not mentioned here, be reflected and meditated upon in the light of one's own feelings and experiences. Become aware of how you respond to them emotionally and what meaning they have for you.

(III) Conclusion, the Ethos of a Support and Supervision Group

If the ethos of a support or supervision group is right, then everything else about the group will come right, or at the very least, have a real possibility of doing so. If it is wrong, then in the end everything will be wrong no matter how much skill and effort is put into trying to make it right. Therefore before moving on to examine other things a very clear definition of the ethos of a group is necessary.

It is now clear that this ethos must most definitely be of the second type of person described by St Augustine as an analogy of the kingdom of God and its values, as we are able to express them at this present time. I see that this is set out very clearly in the Epistle to the Ephesians, Chapter 4 verses 11-16. This has already been quoted in Chapter XI, but it is worth quoting again here for ease of reference.

> And to some, his gift was that they should be apostles; to some, prophets; to some, evangelists; to some, pastors and teachers; so that the saints together make a work of unity in the work of service, building up the body of Christ. In this way we are all to come to unity in our faith and in our knowledge of the Son of God, until we become the perfect Man, fully mature with the fullness of Christ himself.
>
> Then we shall not be children any longer, or tossed one way and another and carried along by every wind of doctrine, at the mercy of all the tricks men play and their cleverness in practising deceit. If we live by the truth and in love, we shall grow in all ways into Christ, who is the head by whom the whole body is fitted and joined together, every joint adding its own strength, for each separate part to work according to its own function. So the body grows until it has built itself up, in love. (JB)

May I now draw out the points made here which show the reasons why a group setting is of much more value in counsellor or pastoral care supervision than one to one situations. I do not wish to make it an either/or issue, but merely to say that a group is better, mainly because it offers a medium in which fuller growth and development of skills can take place. One to one supervision has its place, but on its own it can be dangerous and will never be able to offer enough in the end. These then, are the main points indicating the value of group settings:

(I) Group supervision enlarges the experience of the individuals in it, including the leader
Within any group there would be a variety of skills, experiences, personalities and approaches to problems. These, when accepted, shared, understood and received, would inevitably enrich each individual in the group. In a one to one situation this could not happen, and therefore what the supervised person receives would always be limited, no matter how good the supervisor. With the one to one situation there is also the problem of transference, which could lead to a problem of cloning in which the supervised becomes a replica of the supervisor. The argument that the supervisors are themselves supervised does not help much, because the buck must stop with some individual in the end. This will tend to make some person into 'god' for the system to work, and that person will be put into an untenable position by the pressures of the process. Anyone who could accept this kind of position would be the worst possible kind of person because it has all the ingredients of a power trip, and this is totally opposite to the values of the kingdom of God.

(II) The Holy Spirit can work more effectively in a group in the task of leading us into all truth (St John's Gospel Chapter 16)
This automatically allows into the situation that extra spiritual dimension pertaining to the Kingdom of God that can be experienced within the body of Christ as lived here while on earth. We cannot organize this or in any way make it happen, we can only give the Holy Spirit the space to work, and discern his work when it happens. The function of a leader in such a group is therefore one of enabling the group to function in such a

way as to allow this to happen. The leader must be the one who can provide the security needed for individuals to feel free to be open in the most complete way that they are able.

This would point to four essential qualities in such a person. They are:

(i) Spiritual authority that comes from having a mature faith (1 Timothy Chapter 3 verses 3-7).

(ii) Being experienced and competent in pastoral care and counselling.

(iii) Understanding group dynamics and being practically competent at group leadership.

(iv) Having a well disciplined and well nurtured spiritual life so that he or she is well enough in tune with God to discern where the Spirit is moving.

(III) The purpose of the group must be equally for promoting the spiritual and emotional growth in its members as it is for developing counselling and pastoral skills

To develop counselling and pastoral skills without attention to maturity and spiritual values can become destructive to the point of being evil. When technical skills are developed in people without the corresponding reference to spiritual maturity involving self awareness, together with spiritual and emotional growth, we are in danger of breeding a race of clever tricksters and exploiters, devoid of the grace and humility required to love and respect other people. Nevertheless, we must not let this lead us into despising all forms of secular skills, but accept them, evaluate them carefully and use them whenever it is appropriate to do so.

(IV) The group must be one that strengthens and affirms

The truth must be spoken in love. It is when love is actually experienced and not just talked about that it encourages people and builds them up, giving them the courage to go out and face whatever task is set before them. In the present world, as of old, we are all vulnerable to certain pressures, panics and manipulations that can undermine our self confidence. This is so for counsellors in that they are faced with a very wide, and sometimes conflicting variety of theories, techniques and approaches to the many problems involved. Some are good, some are not, some are just gimmicks and others might work for one person but not another. We need a secure place in which to sort them out for ourselves and test them before we use them with clients. A competent and stable loving group can be the ideal place in which to do this. Such a group allows mistakes to be made, doubts aired, negative emotions to be expressed without any fear of condemnation or rejection, and above all an on-going source of support that is always available. This aspect of a group is one which totally banishes the use of 'empty bombast'.

PROBLEMS GENERALLY FACED BY COUNSELLORS AND PASTORAL CARERS

In this section we look at those problems commonly faced by those who work in any form of pastoral care or counselling. They are the ones for which support is required if they are to offer good quality care and service to their clients and not become bogged down in destructive relationships with them. We will take these problems in order of priority, putting first those issues which, if not attended to very carefully, cause the most damage. Our method is to begin with the base, which underlines all the issues and enables all the others to be dealt with in turn. It is like building up a wall, layer by layer, brick by brick. The foundation must come first and be well laid or else the whole wall will collapse, no matter how good the quality of the bricks.

(i) The problem of personal confidence

This is of the utmost importance. Any pastor or counsellor who is uncertain or anxious, and transmitting panic vibes in the presence of a person who is seeking help will not be of much use to the client. Any skills possessed by the helper, be they natural or the result of training, will be rendered ineffective. There are a number of reasons for lack of confidence, but none of them can be looked at and overcome unless the right kind of support is given. It is a support that is based upon honesty and open loving relationships that can only be experienced within a situation that is created and sustained by a quality group of the ethos we have just described. Real support is the base from which valid and creative supervision can take place. The truth about lack of confidence needs to come out so that it can be overcome, and the worst enemy of this is when people are forced to be defensive because of lack of trust. The group leader must be able to allow such an atmosphere of trust to develop in a group that all the members can feel free to express any emotion they wish, to cry, scream or rage, without any fear of being judged, condemned, or their work written off. Without this quality of support, supervision of cases can become an empty exercise or even destructive.

The questions can be asked, from where does genuine confidence come, and what is it that undermines it? One certain reply to these questions is that it comes from sources not concerned with skills, training, or any form of human natural ability. Very skilled, very highly trained, intelligent and professional people are very vulnerable to lack of confidence, and their hard gained skills do very little to help them in times of crisis. In fact, being professional can make things worse by adding the extra burden of guilt that comes from a feeling that one ought to cope better. It would seem evident, as St Augustine has shown, that the source of our confidence comes from being well sustained, emotionally and spiritually, by good quality loving and accepting relationships in which we can really trust without any fear of being betrayed. Outside the context of such relationships any form of supervision that only seeks to examine skills, check out competence, defend the image of an institution, and train rigorously to maintain standards will become counter productive when it comes down to helping a client.

The work of R R Carkhuff, *Helping and Human Relationships*, demonstrated this point clearly:

> In directly comparable studies selected lay persons, with or without training and/or supervision have had patients who demonstrate change as great or greater than the patients of professional practitioners (p 6).

This shows that there are important factors unrelated to the content of professional training and supervision. He suggests that they are to do with the personal qualities of character which I think can only come about through being so well-sustained through supportive relationships that one is given a positive and realistic personal confidence or OK feeling.

When a support/supervision group is able to sustain this ethos, those who belong are not only given self confidence, but also encouragement to work on their own weakness in an honest way. This in turn gives ability to stay with the pain of clients, accept their negative outbursts, recognise transferences and projections, working with them creatively rather than avoiding them, but above all be able to live gracefully with this world's hurts and failures. There are no professional tricks that help us to do this most essential of caring tasks.

It is one thing to be able to recognise these things and understand them in emotional terms, but it is quite another to live with them and not eventually lose confidence. We have already dealt with the importance of seeking spiritual support, but it is worth mentioning here again the value of Ignatian type spiritual exercises that can be practised in a group as well as individually. Meditations on selected passages from the book of Job, the Servant Songs from Isaiah and Jesus in the Garden of Gethsemane would be good for group use. Again, the need for the group leader to be a competent spiritual director with a sound and mature faith has already been stressed.

Finally, it is important to point out that any sensitive, aware person will be very vulnerable to loss of confidence when engaged in any form of pastoral care or counselling if his or her basic belief is that everything depends on them, their skills, their training, and their strength. But one who has an equal awareness of God at work in the world through the Holy Spirit can indeed have a realistic confidence in the redemptive work of God in Christ that only needs a willing heart on our part. This then puts us in a position where we can let go and let God, but we do need a support group of the right kind to enable us to learn this.

(ii) Unresolved problems in the counsellor

In any counselling dialogue the client has the power to strike off strong emotional reactions in the counsellor. These are nearly always related to unresolved emotional issues from the counsellor's past. They can lead into very dangerous and uncreative situations because they reduce the availability of the counsellor to the client in a way that can bring about change and healing. This strikes at the very heart of good counselling practice.

On the positive side, when a counsellor is able to explore these things by allowing them to be exposed within a supportive and skilled group situation, or in some cases with an individual, it can become a means of growth and development of skills. Many such difficulties can lie dormant within a person for years until set off by a particular situation with a particular person. Such problems are of a very wide and varied nature such as would be impossible to describe here. A common example however, is where a problem being presented is very similar to a past problem in the counsellor which has not been fully resolved. It may be repressed, denied, or even forgotten because the counsellor has never previously been in a situation where it has been re-echoed or exposed.

A group can help the counsellor to become aware of this kind of problem and provide them with the means of resolution. The actual techniques by which this may be achieved will be set out later when we come to the section on technical problems.

(iii) Lack of skills

These lacks in individuals soon become evident when case work is being presented within a well run group. It requires only that the others in the group who have the skills, pass them on. This is a very strong argument in favour of group, rather than individual supervision, but it does show the need for the group to be well set up and wisely led. A good group should always have members with as wide a variety of skills and approaches to counselling as possible, together with a good mix of men and women, age and youth. The leader must be a good enabler, a mature person able to allow everyone to contribute in a relevant way from their skills and experience.

(iv) Lack of a good history of the client

Appendix B in the abridged version of Frank Lake's *Clinical Theology* by Martin Yeomans sets out everything that is required by way of a good history. A counsellor would be well advised to know all this so that in their mind there is a complete list of facts required. However, there is one big pitfall to be avoided, that of going through the list of required information as though it was an inventory, or a checklist of holiday requirements. In a good counselling relationship the client will bring it all out in the order that they find the easiest, the most painful coming last. The order will be different for each client, but the need for a full history is the same in every case.

Failure to obtain a full history lies more with problems in the counsellor of the kind we have already considered than in the counsellor not knowing what information is required. This is because the latter is just a case of learning it, while the former involves deeper and often more painful issues for the counsellor.

The lack of adequate history usually manifests itself in the counsellor with a feeling of being stuck, of frustration, impatience, and eventually a sense of failure or inadequacy. In most cases it is the feelings in the counsellor that make the client feel insecure and so prevent information vital to the counselling process from being given.

This section ends having come full circle. Just the simple matter of a factual case history points back to the deeper and more difficult issues of confidence, the wellbeing of the counsellor and the importance of committed loving support within the context of a group that has a truly creative ethos.

HOW TO SET UP THE GROUP
The diagram on the following page shows how it should be done.

When the group leader is satisfied that enough time has been spent on the case, he/she invites each observer in turn to say what they have observed in the dialogue.

The rest of the group, with the leader as facilitator, now share any insights, observations or questions they have about the case, which in turn helps the Presenter.

At the opening of each session, members are invited to share any

Model for Supervision Group

Real case work is shared in the group, particularly when a counsellor feels 'stuck'. The following model is used.

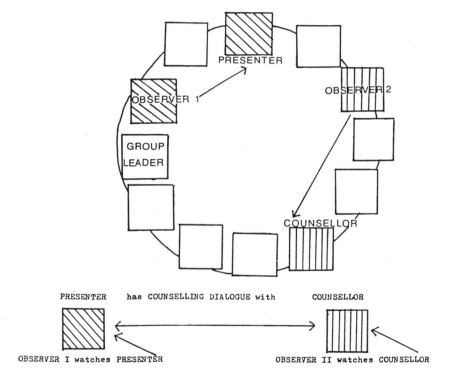

PRESENTER   has COUNSELLING DIALOGUE with   COUNSELLOR

OBSERVER I watches PRESENTER   OBSERVER II watches COUNSELLOR 'feedback' from the last meeting and make bids for time to present a case. The leader then decides who is to be allocated time; on average three can be covered in a session.

The model is mainly self explanatory from a purely practical point of view, but there are several issues which it would be beneficial to discuss further. They are:

(i) The issue of means and ends

The model demonstrates a means whereby a group can be organised for a specific purpose. If the achievement of a perfectly working model is all that is sought, then games can be played over technicalities that will result in squashing any possibility of creative work. The group leader, therefore, must always have the end, objectives of the group, clearly in mind. These objectives are, firstly to help everyone in the group to feel secure, relaxed and accepted. This in turn will create the correct ethos in which everyone feels able to be honest about their failings without any threat to their personal integrity. Secondly, whenever any material comes up, be it technicalities such as lack of appropriate skills, personal pain that surfaces as a result of a counselling dialogue, or just lack of confidence brought about by a difficult client, it must be able to be dealt with honestly and with integrity. All the following issues are ones that arise out of these two points.

(ii) The dynamics of the group

These are important for two reasons. Firstly, it is by allowing a healthy dynamic to develop out of the ethos described earlier that enables each individual member to contribute fully out of his or her own skills and insights. When this happens everyone is enriched and the experience of each member is extended. An example of this happening is when one member presents a case of the type that nobody else has experienced. A leader who is able to allow a free flow of comments, questions and explorations to take place with other members of the group taking over the leadership temporarily where they have the required skills and insights, will allow this enrichment to happen. An insecure or not very competent leader will not be able to do this and the quality of the group will suffer.

It is also true that a good and competent leader will also allow himself or herself to become enriched by a group with a good dynamic. This demonstrates the Gospel truth: 'For to everyone who has will be given more, and he will have more than enough; but from the man who has not, even what he has will be taken away' (Matthew Chapter 13, verse 12, JB).

Secondly, the leader must be familiar with the workings of the Holy Spirit, so that there is an awareness of his presence in the group. This extra dimension allows more openness because it brings more things to light. When this is so there is both more pain and more blessing, but the greatest gain is that real prayer is possible, and not prayer that is just an empty gesture because it covers up and avoids facing deeper issues that are painful, and in the eyes of the faithless, very threatening. The Holy Spirit does need a good dynamic to operate in the first instant. It is therefore important that a leader should have the right skills to create this, but it must never be an end in itself, because there is always much more reality than this. The reality of God the Holy Spirit at work leads beyond that which is possible in merely human terms and needs to be experienced to be understood.

(iii) The support aspect of the group

This is mainly to encourage personal growth and as a result of this greater counselling and pastoral competence. For this to happen it is important that each group session opens with a time of sharing. When this is done a sense of continuation develops that helps the dynamic of the group and gives each member a special feeling of belonging, so that when they are out doing their work between meetings, an awareness develops that they are not alone but in a continuing relationship with a source of sustenance that is specially there for them. From this a commitment develops to the group as well as a commitment of the group to its individual members.

Two things are important in the sharing process. The first one is to share at the very beginning how each member feels, where they are in overall terms of their life and work at the present moment, sad, happy, tired, frustrated, angry etc. Each person shares in this manner and other members are invited to respond freely whenever anything comes up which strikes a chord in them. It is important that time is rationed appropriately, and, as far as possible, according to need. There may be times when most of the group session is taken up with the distress of just one member. In such cases, which are rare, it is important that the whole group agrees that it is the appropriate thing to do this.

The second kind of sharing is feedback. This is when members report back to the group in the present session with cases which they presented previously at group sessions. This is only done when an individual wishes. Reasons for doing so are either to say that all is well and that the help offered the group was beneficial, or to ask the group for further help.

(iv) Bidding for time

This always follows the initial time of sharing and is a way of allocating time for group members to work on cases or their own agenda according to need. The leader is responsible for allocating time after consultation with group members. For a case study the system is set up according to the diagram 'Model for a Supervision Group'. Both individual counselling cases and pastoral situations can be studied using this method. Anything else that comes up in the group which seems important for the development, growth and general wellbeing of individual members can be dealt with in whatever way the group thinks is appropriate.

Sometimes a member has some special skill or insight to share, and at other times prayer, or any other exercise that develops skills, awareness or spiritual and emotional growth, such as fantasy journeys, can be used. These should always be done in a relaxed and informal manner. If the tensions are high following a difficult case presentation, which may have involved the exposure of pain or exhaustion due to much energy having been used, it is wise to have a break for tea or coffee with a relaxed chat, before settling down to further work. Pushing ourselves too hard with difficult cases and situations can become destructive and is often a cover up for anxiety based in lack of trust that God is able to do what we cannot and should not be expected to do.

(v) A final point

It must be stressed that confidentiality is of the utmost importance. Everything shared within the group is the property of the group and must not be discussed outside it. Only a group in which there is a high level of confidentiality and trust will be able to carry out its purpose properly.

EPILOGUE

In drawing to a close this section on groups and group leadership, it would be apt to come to some conclusions. The practice of leaving everything open-ended tends to be uncreative; it gives nobody the stimulus to disagree or be provoked into making their own discoveries. Four very definite conclusions can be drawn for the purpose just stated – two arising from the material presented in this work, and two arising from how these conclusions relate to the author's observations of the present situation in our churches.

The conclusions are, firstly, that groups will form themselves anyway because of the nature of things. Those concerned with the running and leadership of groups are not therefore engaged in organising something *ex nihilo* so to speak, but managing or 'farming' what is already potentially there. It is true that some groups can be dangerous, having a negative influence on members, and this is especially true of some that form themselves as C S Lewis points out in *The Inner Ring*, but they are the weeds that good farming by those in a position of pastoral responsibility can control if they have the know-how.

Secondly, the quality of the leadership is the most important factor in the health of a small group. This means that leadership involves more than learning techniques or 'knowing how to do it'. The leader must be a person with a high degree of authority which the group accepts and respects. This points to a high degree of maturity in such a person. Time and chronological age are required to achieve it, but they do not always guarantee it. Such leadership involves the extra dimension of 'being' a certain type of person, one with a balance between knowing how to do it, and one whose being is such that it transmits a sense of safety and security to others. Such a person has a kind of neutrality that allows others freedom to be themselves, and indeed has the spiritual and emotional maturity that was described by Erikson, as 'generativity'. This, as we have seen, describes a person who is able to give freely of themselves from their experience without the need to prove anything for themselves; a 'no strings attached' person who is not easily threatened by whatever other people are or do. Again, may I point you to 1 Timothy Chapter 3 verses 4-7, when it describes the kind of person suitable to be an elder in the Church:

> He must be a man who manages his own family well and brings his children up to obey him and be well behaved: how can a man who does not know how to manage his own family have responsibility for the church of God? He should not be a new convert in case pride should turn his head and then he might be condemned as the devil was condemned. It is also necessary that people outside the church should speak well of him, so that he never gets a bad reputation and falls into the devil's trap (JB).

Thirdly, how are such people produced? The simple answer is that in the right milieu they just grow, and these people with the correct talents will become obvious. The problem is that in Britain at the present time the churches do not often provide the right milieu for spiritual growth and maturity. There is too much pressure, especially upon clergy, pushing them into activities that are administrative in nature and amount to keeping the system going with no time for anything else. People who are so pressured become exhausted and in order to survive have to build stony defences against recognising and working with their own basic emotions such as feelings of anxiety, anger, lust and despair. It is in recognising and working with such things and allied matters that people grow emotionally and spiritually into the kind of people who will make good group leaders. There are no short cuts, and in falling into the temptation of taking such short cuts as might appear suitable to those under administrative pressure, the end product tends to be someone who is clever, and has a bag of tricks that looks good, but is basically incompetent and dangerous. Such people have hurt many and put them off groups thereby denying them a source of support that they need.

Finally: if groups are important for the purpose of emotional and spiritual growth, and if such things are essential for the church's life, it could be argued that the present situation within the local church structure is such that it does not provide the milieu for healthy church life. This is because, by its very nature it does not provide the environment in which the necessary spiritual leadership can be developed.

It would appear that in such a situation, God in his sovereign power can and does act to provide the right environment outside those established structures. Such a milieu has always been provided by movements and communities that are outside them, but within the body spiritual. This is a well established theological principle concerning the way in which God works to sustain the faith of his people, and is rooted in the very creative 'Prophet/Priest' tension of the Old Testament. A good example of this can be seen in the book of Amos, especially in the confrontation between Amos the prophet and Amaziah the priest (Amos Chapter 7, verses 10-17). The issue here was that the priest was busily maintaining a system of worship and ministry which had become all consuming and hidebound. It was not meeting the spiritual needs of the people, but it worked well enough for Amaziah and those within it. It also blinded them to greater spiritual issues, rendering them quite spiritually ineffectual. From within this system, even though it contained truth, it was impossible to bring about the reform that was needed so that its truths could be made readily available. An outside agent, who was at the same time one of the faithful and in some kind of sympathy with the truths that lay buried within the system, had to come and confront it. Hence Amos, faithful Israelite but not a priest, a man outside the system, was raised up by God to save the truths enshrined within the system.

This is, of course, no strange thing in the history of the Church. The whole of the monastic movement can be seen as 'prophetic', beginning with the move out into the desert by people like St Anthony, to find time and space to get near to God. This happened against the background of a collapsing Roman Empire. Also movements inspired by people such as St Francis of Assisi and St Teresa of Avila are later examples of this same thing, as are Charles de Foucauld and Mother Teresa of Calcutta in more modern times.

Yet another example of this, which is not monastic, is the 18th century Methodist movement led by John Wesley. The history of The Methodist Movement also shows how over a period of time a movement that was originally prophetic can become over systematized and moribund. I get this complaint often from Methodists who feel frustrated by the bureaucracy of modern Methodism. It seems that through the operation of the Holy Spirit, God continues this process of breaking down and rebuilding, (see Jeremiah Chapter 1, verses 9-10) and will do so until the end of this age comes.

Within the modern church there are a multiplicity of movements, so much so, that one suspects that in the modern age God's activity would indicate a renewal of prophetic activity. If this is true, God is providing a milieu in which those who will be suitable for small group leadership can be nurtured. This activity is in the prophetic stream of the Church's life rather than the priestly one.

We must therefore take a look at movements, groups and communities outside the church's official structures to see if they can provide some of the help required for people's emotional and spiritual growth. There is evidence that this is happening from the growth of movements and communities in Britain during the second half of this century. Dr David Clarke has studied this development and as a result of his work a Centre has been set up in Birmingham to monitor and assist these groups. It is a very valuable resource for anyone interested or involved in them. The name and address of the centre is:- The National Association of Christian Communities and Networks, 1046 Bristol Road, Birmingham B29 6LJ. Tel. 0121 472 8079.

In conclusion, when taking a look at the influence small groups can have, it is important to see them always within the wider context of the structures of sociology as well as history. Small groups are the inspiration of the larger structure – the leaven in the dough.

The kingdom of heaven is like leaven which a woman took and hid
in three measures of meal, till it was all leavened
(Matthew, Chapter 13, verse 33).

The Counsellor's Relationship with God

Further suggested reading

The Confessions	St Augustine	Penguin Classics
Knowing God	J I Packer	Hodder and Stoughton
Sadhana, a way to God	A de Mello	Gujurat Sahitya Prakash, Anand, India
Seeking God	E de Waal	Collins, Fount Paperbacks
Be still and know	M Ramsay	Collins, Fount Paperbacks
Celebration of Discipline	Richard Foster	Hodder and Stoughton
Reaching out	Henri J Nouwen	Collins, Fount Paperbacks
The Heart in Pilgrimage	C Bryant	DLT
Exploration into Contemplative Prayer	H Slade	DLT
The Practice of the Presence of God	Brother Laurence	Hodder Paperback
Fully Human, Fully Alive and Unconditional Love	J Powell	Argus Communications
Spiritual Pilgrims	J Welch	Paulist Press

Your Dreams, God's Neglected Gift	Herman Riffel	Kingsway
A Grove Booklet on Dreams	Russ Parker	Grove Books Ltd. Ridley Hall Road, Cambridge CB3 9HU
Keeping Your Personal Journal	George Simons	Paulist Press
Your Life in Your Hands	Brian Hawker	Fount

The Counsellor and the Family

Bibliography

Attachment and Loss (3 volumes)	Bowlby J	Penguin 1984/1985
Marriage, Faith and Love	Dominian J	Collins/Fount 1984
Marital Therapy in Britain (2 volumes)	Dryden W (ed)	Harper and Row 1985
The Art of Loving	Fromm E	Unwin Paperbacks 1975
Once Upon a Group	Kindred M	(From the author at 20, Dover St. Southwell, Notts. NG25 OEZ)
Love and Anger in Marriage	Mace D	Zondervan, 1972
Families and How to Survive Them	Skynner R and Cleese J	Methuen 1983
T.A. Today, A New introduction to Transactional Analysis	Stewart I and Joines U	Lifespace Pubs. Nottingham and Chapel Hill
Inner Work, using dreams and active imagination for personal growth	Johnson Robert A	Harper, San Francisco

Marriage Difficulties	Tournier P	Highland Books 1984
Families Matter	Whitfield R (ed)	Marshall Pickering 1987
Community and Growth	Vanier Jean	DLT

A Short List of Voluntary Helping Agencies for Families

The majority of voluntary agencies offer their services freely and confidentially. When required, payment is usually for specialist advice following a free introductory session.

For details of services in your area, contact your local Council for Voluntary Service, Community Service or Rural Community Council. Their numbers will be in the phone book under the city or county in which you live.

Citizens Advice Bureau
Offers advice on any subject, personal, family matters, housing, legal. Headquarters: The National Association for Citizens Advice Bureaux, 115/123 Pentonville Road, London N1 9LZ

The British Association for Counselling
Advises on counselling as an activity.
BAC 37a, Sheep Street, Rugby, Warwickshire CV21 3BX (Tel. Rugby 78328/9)

The Association of Christian Counsellors
173a Wokingham Road, Reading, Berks. RG6 1LT (Tel: 01734 662207)

Parents Under Stress
Friendship and support. Local group information from:
OPUS, c/o 223 Westgate Street, Guiseborough, Cleveland TS14 6NJ

Exploring Parenthood
Runs courses and workshops for improving understanding and skills.
Exploring Parenthood, Omnibus Workspace, 39-41 North Road, London N7 9DP

National Children's Home/Family Network
Children's homes and Family centres in large cities.

Phone-in help line service at headquarters.
85, Highbury Park, London N5 1UD
National Children's Centre
Advice and Information with a national register of parent self-help groups.
The Brian Jackson Centre, New North Parade, Huddersfield, West Yorkshire HD1 5JP
Tel: 01484 519988

Samaritans
Friends to people who feel desperate, lonely and suicidal.
Local branches under 'Samaritans' in phone book.
Headquarters: Samaritans Incorporated, 17, Uxbridge Road, Slough, Bucks SL1 1SN

Death and Bereavement
CRUSE – the National Organisation for the Widowed and their Children
Counselling, practical advice and social activities
126, Sheen Road, Richmond, Surrey TW9 IUR

Housing Advice Centres
Most local authorities run a specialist housing advice service.
A list of housing aid or advice centres is available within the London area from SHAC, 189a Old Brompton Road, London SW5 OAR, and outside London from Shelter, 157 Waterloo Road, London SE1 8UU

Legal Advice Centres
Essentially for advice, no charge for service
The Legal Action Group, 242 Pentonville Road, N1 9UN

Relate Marriage Guidance Councils (National network)
Local branches under 'Marriage Guidance' in phone book.
Headquarters: The Relate National Marriage Guidance Council, Herbert Grey College, Little Church Street, Rugby, Warwickshire CV21 3AP

Catholic Marriage Advisory Council
Local centres to counsel couples with marital relationship difficulties, including non-Catholics
15, Lansdowne Road, London W11 3AJ

Conciliation services
The National Family Conciliation Council, 34 Milton Road, Swindon, Wilts SN1 5AJ

Divorce, Separation, Stepfamilies

Gingerbread
Self help groups for single parents; services include baby-sitting, play school and holiday schemes, crisis support, phone-in service.
35, Wellington Street, London WC2E 7BN
39, Hope Street, Glasgow G3
171, University Street, Belfast BT7

National Stepfamily Association
Help, advice, information.
Maris House, Maris Lane, Trumpington, Cambridgeshire

Families need Fathers
Concerned with problems of maintaining a child's relationship with both its parents following separation and divorce. Support and help for men and women with access and custody problems.
37, Carden Road, London SE15 3UB

Addiction
Alcoholics Anonymous
Mutual support groups of men and women
11, Redcliffe Gardens, London SW10 9BG

Al-Anon Family Groups
For relatives and friends of problem drinkers
61, Great Dover Street, London SE1 4YF
Alateen
For teenagers with alcoholic friends or relatives
61, Great Dover Street, London SE1 4YF

Gamblers Anonymous
Mutual support groups
17/23 Blantyre Street, Cheyne Walk, London SW10

Spirituality

The Vision
A magazine of The National Retreat Association that lists Retreat Houses and Spirituality Centres.
Address: The Central Hall, 256 Bermondsey Street, London SE1 3JU.
Tel: 0171 357 7736
Fax: 1071 357 7724